ISBN 0-75257-665-8

© February 2002, Chronosports Editeur
Jordils Park, Chemin des Jordils 40, CH-1025 St-Sulpice, Switzerland. Tel: +41 (0)21 694 24 44. Fax: +41 (0)21 694 24 46.

This is a Parragon Book

This edition published in 2002

Parragon
Queen Street House
4 Queen Street
Bath BA1 1HE, UK

Copyright © Parragon

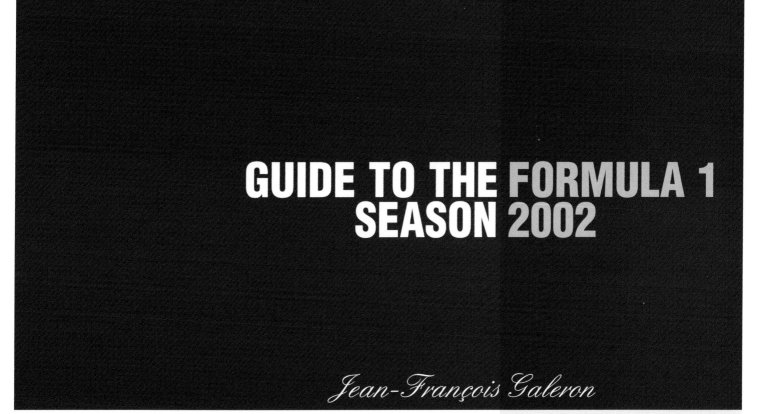

# GUIDE TO THE FORMULA 1 SEASON 2002

*Jean-François Galeron*

**Paste-up and layout** *Cyril Davillerd*
**Coordination** *Vincent Souchaud*

# CONTENTS

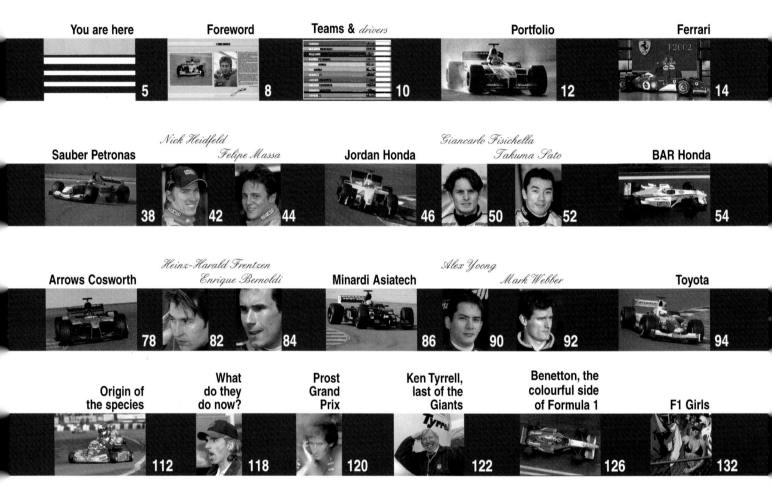

*Born on September 27, 1957 in Lyon, Jean-François Galeron studied law before opting for a complete change of direction, becoming a motorsport photographer, almost by accident, at the end of the Seventies.*
*He quickly chose to specialise in Formula One. So far, he has attended over 300 Grands Prix and he is part of a small group of French photographers who attend all F1 events. He works with major specialist magazines in France, Germany, Japan, England and Portugal. Since 1989, at first as a photographer, he has contributed to this book which presents the coming F1 season. Since 1995, he has taken over the writing duties.*
*With other publishers, he has also produced biographies of Alain Prost, Ayrton Senna, Damon Hill, Jean Alesi, Jacques Villeneuve, Michael Schumacher and Mika Häkkinen. As for more general themes, he has produced "Ten years of F1 Racing", "Girls in Racing", and "Formula 1 in the Paddock", in 2001. Finally, since 2000 he has produced a book which gathers his best photos of the year, called "Formule 1 - Emotions".*

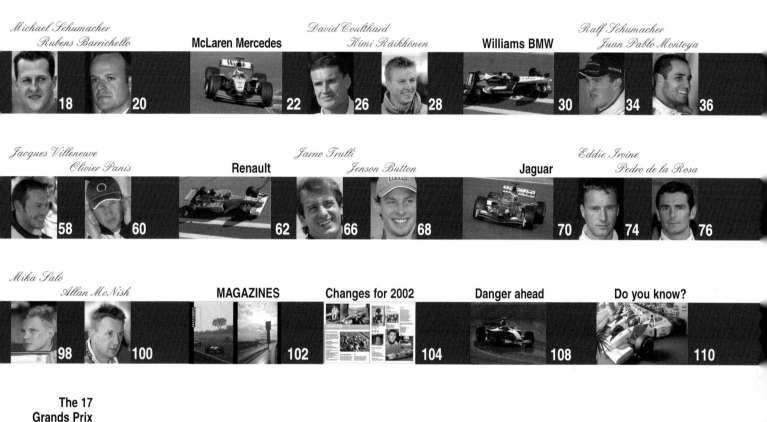

*Jean-François Galeron*
*would like to thank all the drivers who answered his questions and*
*have put up with his flash guns over the years.*
*The team press officers and personnel made his work much easier.*
*Since 1984, Jean-Francois Galeron has used Canon equipment.*
*Jfg@galeron.com*

# FOREWORD

Thursday January 31, 2002 is a great day for me. Here, at the Barcelona circuit, I have just completed my first day of testing at the wheel of the Renault R 202. I am very happy and optimistic about the future. I think it will take me a few months to settle in to my new world. I have discovered that the new Renault team is extremely motivated. That's fantastic, because I feel the same way.

I have been karting since the age of eight and racing is my whole life. I hope this year will be a turning point in my career. It is the first time I am driving for a major team, with the strength and power of a major manufacturer behind me. I have kept some wonderful memories of my years with Minardi, Prost and Jordan. Unfortunately, we never really had the means to fight for victory.

Despite that, I have had a good time, even though I was often sidelined by reliability issues. But I am not complaining. I now have the chance to work with a major player. Right from my first contact with the people at Renault, I have been impressed by the attention to detail displayed by the engineers in the way they listen to my comments. I had never experienced that in the past. I feel I am here to help the team progress. As Patrick Faure made clear on the day of the presentation, I know it will take time before we can win with a new car, a new engine and some futuristic ideas. But I am confident. This is an exciting challenge and it will be fascinating. We are starting from nothing with a clean sheet of paper.

I am aware that it will be difficult for me to win races this year. I think the title fight will come down to a battle between Ferrari, McLaren and Williams. Behind this trio, Renault, Sauber, Jordan and BAR will fight over fourth place in the championship and it will be very close.

My team-mate, Jenson Button, shares my sense of motivation. We have to help the team progress and try and pick up a few podium finishes.

I am very happy to write the preview for Jean-Francois Galeron's book. I have nicknamed him "Gaga" ever since he came to visit me in Pescara in 1998!

"Guide to the Formula 1 Season 2002" really lets you get to know everything about the teams, drivers, circuits, statistics and all the little foibles of this strange world which has been my home for the past six years.

Jarno Trulli, January 31, 2002

# FERRARI

## McLAREN MERCEDES

## WILLIAMS BMW

## SAUBER PETRONAS

## JORDAN HONDA

## BAR HONDA

## RENAULT F1

## JAGUAR COSWORTH

## ARROWS COSWORTH

## MINARDI ASIATECH

## TOYOTA F1

# SCUDERIA **FERRARI**MARLBORO

# SCUDERIA FERRARI

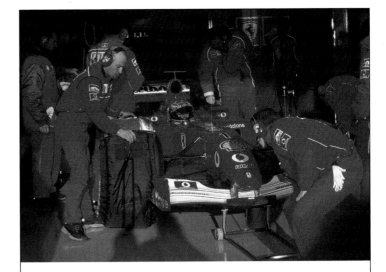

"For the first time in eleven years, I couldn't ask the team to do better than last year," said Ferrari's President, Luca di Montezemolo, at the launch of the Maranello team's latest challenger. "I will accept the same result as last year."

After three consecutive Constructors' titles, and two in a row Drivers' titles, the president is being generous. Another drivers title would be Michael Schumacher's fifth, equalling the record of Juan Manuel Fangio, no mean feat in these ultra-competitive days.

But once again, the Jean Todt-led team isn't resting on its laurels in 2002. Far from it. While there is considerable stability within the Scuderia in personnel terms, its engineers have come up with much innovation in a year when others teams have been largely stagnant in terms of radical, new designs, due to absence of change in the regulations. "Innovation", "revised", "reviewed", "new materials" were all much-used expressions describing the new car from Rory Byrne. There is a completely new transmission for the first time in several years, designed in synergy with the revised 051 engine, an improvement on the championship winning 050.

Ferrari are also maximising their close relationship with their Bridgestone tyre supplier, now that they are the Japanese company's indisputable top team following McLaren's defection to Michelin.

They had just 15 days to prove the new car - but still had the safety net of the 2001 car. Whatever they use, they would be hard to catch.

## Scuderia Ferrari Marlboro

Address: Gestione Sportiva
Scuderia Ferrari Marlboro,
Via Ascari 55/57,
41053 Maranello (Mo), Italy
Tel: +39 0536 94 94 50
Fax: +39 0536 94 94 36
Internet: www.ferrari.it

Sporting Director: Jean Todt
Technical Director: Ross Brawn
Number of staff: 681

GP debut: Monaco 1950
Number of GP participations: 653
First win: Great Britain 1951 (Gonzales)
Number of wins: 144
Number of pole positions: 148
Number of fastest race laps: 147
Total points score: 2,659.5
Points average per race: 4.07

Constructors' World titles: 11 (1961, 64, 75, 76, 77, 79, 82, 83, 99, 2000 and 2001).
Drivers' world titles: 11 (Ascari: 1952 and 1953, Fangio: 1956, Hawthorn: 1958, P. Hill: 1961, Surtees: 1964, Lauda: 1975 and 1977, Scheckter: 1979 and M. Schumacher: 2000 and 2001)

Test drivers: Luca Badoer (Italy) and Luciano Burti (Brazil)

2001 classification: Drivers' and Constructors' World Champions

### The 2001 season summary...

- Constructors' World Champions
- 9 wins (Schumacher)
- 11 pole positions (Schumacher)
- 3 fastest race laps (Schumacher)
- 179 points scored (Schumacher 123, Barrichello 56)
- 28 Grands Prix finishes from 34 starts (Schumacher 15, Barrichello 13)
- 28 points-scoring Grand Prix finishes

### Strong points

- On a winning streak.
- Huge motivation.
- Colossal budget.
- Presence of Michael Schumacher, the best driver in the world.
- Excellent technical staff.
- Bridgestone's only front running team.

### Weak points

- It can sometimes be harder to stay at the top than to get there.
- Bridgestone's only front running team.
- Innovative new car lacks testing.
- Occasionally beaten on strategy.
- The whole team revolves around Schumacher.

Jean Todt

Ross Brawn

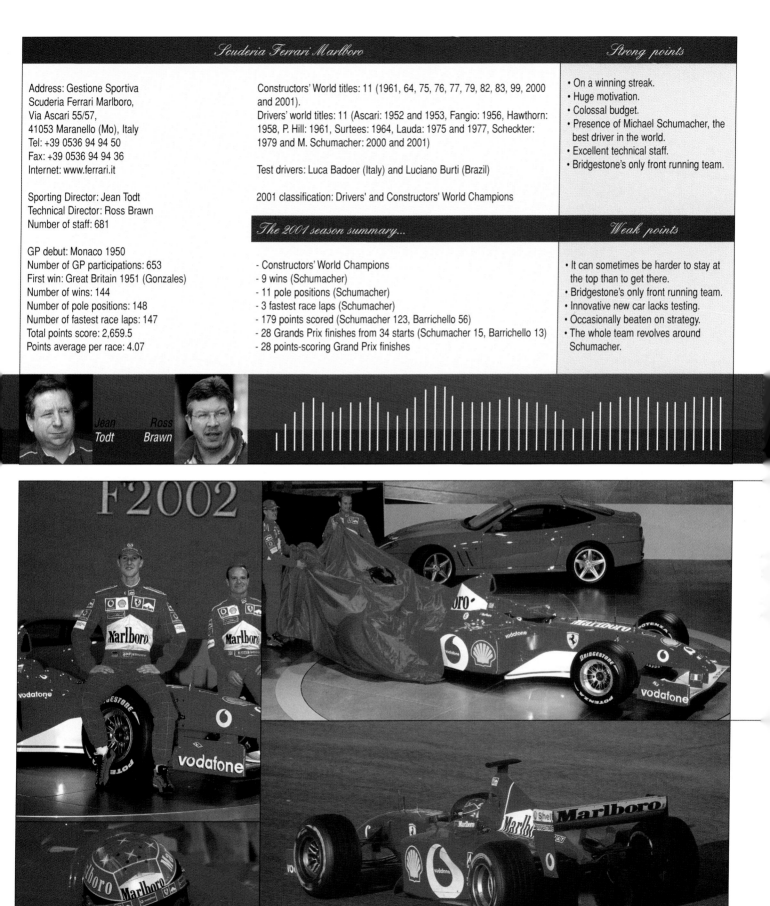

F2002

# MICHAELSCHUMACHER

## *Ferrari*

It is hard to find new superlatives to describe Michael Schumacher's performance. With four titles already in the bag, it is equally hard to see who can stop him from pocketing some more. Scuderia Ferrari is on a roll, still hungry for success and would seem to be the ideal weapon for him.

The four-times world champion is under contract to the Scuderia to the end of 2004. He recently declared he did not intend hanging up his helmet at that date, but that he had no intention of switching teams. With Ferrari since 1996, he plans to end his career with the team which has given him so much. There were rumours doing the rounds over the winter that he might retire at the end of 2002, with a fifth title in the bag, handing over his seat to Juan Pablo Montoya. He officially denied this story. "I was born on four wheels. I love racing and I don't see any reason to stop." For his part, Jean Todt stated that he would be happy to keep his driver for a further ten years, if he was still in good physical shape. Michael Schumacher is at the height of his powers. His name is at the top of the list for all the various grand prix statistics. Journalists still strive to uncover every facet of this man, to decide if he really is the greatest driver of all time in Formula 1.

This year, he could equal Juan Manuel Fangio's incredible record of five titles. If that happens, it is easy to see him go for one more, which would certainly shut up his detractors, who have never forgotten his wheel-banging incidents with Damon Hill and Jacques Villeneuve.

He will no doubt make it a matter of honour to try and get close to the record for pole positions held by Ayrton Senna, a driver he admired and modelled himself on. If he does go on to take this prestigious record, it will no doubt be an emotional moment for him. We are lucky enough to be here to witness this exceptional champion's exploits. Where will it end?

# Michael Schumacher

Date and place of birth: January 3, 1969 in Hürth-Hermühlheim (Germany)
Nationality: German
Lives: Vufflens-le-Château (Switzerland)
Marital status: Married to Corinna, two children (Gina Maria and Mick)
Height: 1,74 m    Weight: 75 kg

Internet: www.michael-schumacher.de

## Career summary

Racing debut: 1973 (karts)
GP debut: Belgium 1991 (Jordan)

162 Grands Prix
801 points scored
Points average per GP: 4.94
96 podiums
53 wins
29 second places
14 third places
6 fourth places
6 fifth places
4 sixth places
43 pole positions
44 fastest race laps

Qualifying score in 2001:
Schumacher 16 / Barrichello 1

Titles:
Two-times German Kart champion in 1984 and 1985.
German Formula König champion in 1988.
German F3 champion in 1990.
Four-times F1 world champion in 1994 and 95 (Benetton), 2000 and 2001 (Ferrari).

## F1 Record

Best classification in F1: World Champion in 1994 and 95 (Benetton), 2000 and 2001 (Ferrari)
Best GP result: 1st (53 wins)
Best qualification in F1: 1st (43 pole positions)

1991: Jordan and Benetton, 4 points, 12th
1992: Benetton, 53 points, 3rd
1993: Benetton, 52 points, 4th
1994: Benetton, 92 points, World Champion
1995: Benetton, 102 points, World Champion
1996: Ferrari, 49 points, 3rd
1997: Ferrari, 78 points, (excluded from championship)
1998: Ferrari, 86 points, 2nd
1999: Ferrari, 44 points, 5th
2000: Ferrari, 108 points, World Champion
2001: Ferrari, 123 points, World Champion

F1 team-mates:
1991: A. De Cesaris (Jordan)
        and N. Piquet (Benetton)
1992: M. Brundle
1993: R. Patrese
1994: J.J. Lehto, J. Verstappen and J. Herbert
1995: J. Herbert
1996, 1997, 1998 and 1999: E. Irvine
2000 and 2001: R. Barrichello

**First car driven?**
A Fiat 500, when I was 8. The first time I drove it, my foot slipped off the clutch pedal. We were parked in front of a wall. Luckily my father pulled the handbrake on in time.
**Road car?**
A Maserati 3200 GT and the new little Fiat Stilo Abarth, which I use on the numerous occasions I am at Fiorano, a Lancia Zeta, a Ferrari 550 Maranello and... a Fiat 500, which was a present from President Montezemolo.
**Favourite or dream car?**
The Ferrari 550 Barchetta.
**Best race car?**
The 1994 Benetton and the 2001 Ferraris. If I had to pick just one, it would be the one I used in Japan last year.
**Worst race car?**
The 1996 Ferrari F 310.
**Best racing memory?**
Suzuka in 2000 was definitely the best race of my career. The emotion of taking the title with Ferrari in Japan is an unforgettable memory.
**Worst racing memory?**
Imola 1994, and my collision with Villeneuve in Jerez in 1997.
**Your racing ambition?**
To win as many races as possible. Nothing else matters.
**Your favourite circuit?**
Spa is my favourite track.
**Your least favourite circuit?**
None.
**Your favourite driver of all time?**
Ayrton Senna.
**Your favourite driver of the current batch?**
My brother. You cannot be friends with everyone.
**Favourite dish?**
Italian cuisine and spaghetti, especially with tomatoes.
**Favourite drink?**
Apple juice with sparkling water.
**Sports you participate in?**
I discovered climbing about a year ago. I still play football with FC Aubonne. I do a lot of training, jogging, scuba diving, skiing, cycling and mountain-biking.
**Favourite sport?**
I like all sports.
**Favourite sports star?**
I have a lot of respect and admiration for decathletes and triathletes. They are all-round sports people. I also like soccer player Gabriele Battistutta.
**What are your hobbies and interests outside sport?**
Being with Corinna and the children. I like filming them. I collect watches, mainly Omegas. I also like karaoke.
**Favourite films?**
I really enjoy the cinema and I regret not being able to go more often. Recently, I've watched a lot of Disney Club with the children.
**Favourite actor?**
Jodie Foster, Meryl Streep, Nicolas Cage and Anthony Hopkins.
**What do you watch on TV?**
The news and good political debates.
**Favourite music?**
Phil Collins, Tina Turner, Michael Jackson. I also like listening to chill-out music and natural sounds.
**Favourite reading matter?**
Detective stories.
**What is your favourite holiday destination?**
I enjoy going to Utah in the United States and, in the winter, to our chalet in Trysil in Norway.
**Favourite shopping city?**
I don't have a preference.
**Do you have any pets?**
I have 4 dogs, 2 horses and 2 ponies.
**Outside of motorsport, do you admire anyone in particular?**
People like triathletes.
**If you were on a desert island, what would you take with you?**
My wife Corinna and my two children.
**Your ideal day?**
It would need to be longer than 24 hours. It would start with a good night's sleep, a gentle wake-up call, the kids playing on the bed, having time to do some sport and spending time with Corinna and the children.
**What would you do if you were not a racing driver?**
I think I would have been a car mechanic.
**What is the most important thing in life?**
My family.
**What do you like most about your job?**
Working with my team, making progress, winning.
**What are your main strengths?**
I don't like talking about them!
**Have you got any faults?**
That's up to you to say!
**Have you thought about your retirement from racing?**
There is nothing I like more or do better than racing. I don't know when I will retire nor what I will do after that.

# RUBENS BARRICHELLO ② 

*Ferrari*

During Ferrari's traditional pre-season ski week, organised by Marlboro at Madonna di Campiglio, in the Dolomites, Rubens Barrichello seemed happy and relaxed. Having spent over two months with his wife Silvana, watching their son Eduardo growing up, the Brazilian driver was burning with the desire to get back behind the wheel of a Ferrari. He admits, without hesitation, that it's not easy being Michael Schumacher's team-mate. There is a hint of bitterness in his voice, as he recognises the fact that Scuderia Ferrari is built around the four-times world champion.

However, on several occasions last year, he was in a position to win grands prix. In Austria, he had to let his team-mate pass. In Monza and Indianapolis, bad luck robbed him of a deserved victory. In the end, the lack of results prevented him from getting ahead of David Coulthard for the runner-up position in the 2001 championship.

Totally motivated, as he starts his third season with Ferrari, Rubens Barrichello wants to give his very best. He is also happy about the arrival of his best friend, Luciano Burti, as test driver with the team.

The Brazilian knows he can count on the support of Jean Todt, who never forgets to mention what an important contribution Barrichello has made to Ferrari's triumphal progress. 2002 will be an important year, in regards to his future. His contract will expire at the end of the season and no doubt there are many who would like his seat. Up against the Schumacher effect, he has come out of this difficult role with honour. It's not easy to shine when you are up against the best driver in the world.

If he strikes a lucky seam, he has all the qualities to improve his track record, which does not really reflect his ability.

## Rubens Barrichello

Date and place of birth: May 23, 1972 in Sao Paolo (Brazil)
Nationality: Brazilian
Lives: Monte Carlo
Marital status: Married to Silvana, one child (Eduardo)
Height: 1,72 m    Weight: 78 kg

Internet: www.barrichello.com.br

### Career summary

Racing debut: 1981 (karts)
GP debut: South Africa 1993

147 Grands Prix
195 points scored
Points average per GP: 1.32
25 podiums
1 win
11 second places
13 third places
13 fourth places
12 fifth places
4 sixth places
3 pole positions
3 fastest race laps

Qualifying score in 2001: Barrichello 1 / Schumacher 16

Titles:
Five-times Brazilian kart champion from 1981 to 1988.
Opel Lotus Euroseries champion in 1990.
British F3 champion in 1991.

### F1 Record

Best classification in F1: 3rd in 2001 (Ferrari)
Best GP result: 1st (Germany 2000)
Best qualification in F1: 1st (3 pole positions)

1993: Jordan, 2 points, 17th
1994: Jordan, 19 points, 6th
1995: Jordan, 11 points, 11th
1996: Jordan, 14 points, 8th
1997: Stewart, 6 points, 14th
1998: Stewart, 4 points, 14th
1999: Stewart, 21 points, 7th
2000: Ferrari, 62 points, 4th
2001: Ferrari, 56 points, 3rd

F1 team-mates:
1993: I. Capelli, T. Boutsen, E. Naspetti, M. Apicella and E. Irvine
1994 and 1995: E. Irvine
1996: M. Brundle and J. Magnussen
1997: J. Magnussen and J. Verstappen
1999: J. Herbert
2000 and 2001: M. Schumacher

**First car driven?**
An old GM, when I was six.
**Road car?**
A Maserati 3200 GT and a Fiat Stilo Abarth in Italy, and Alfa Romeos when I travel in Europe.
**Favourite or dream car?**
Ferraris are dream cars.
**Best race car?**
All the Ferrari Formula 1 cars I have driven.

**Worst race car?**
The 1998 Stewart.
**Best racing memory?**
My first grand prix win at Hockenheim in 2000.
**Worst racing memory?**
Imola 1994 will always be a nightmare.
**Your racing ambition?**
To be world champion.
**Your favourite circuit?**
Interlagos in Brazil.
**Your least favourite circuit?**
All circuits have some good points.
**Your favourite driver of all time?**
Ayrton Senna and Jackie Stewart.
**Your favourite driver of the current batch?**
Luciano Burti is my best friend, so I am delighted he is now working at Ferrari.
**Favourite dish?**
Pasta.
**Favourite drink?**
Red Bull.

**Sports you participate in?**
Jogging, squash, jet-ski, golf. I have also tried a bit of skiing and snowboarding at Madonna di Campiglio.
**Favourite sport?**
Football, jet-ski and motorcycle grands prix.
**Favourite sports star?**
The Brazilian tennis player, Gustavo Kuerten and Ronaldo, with whom I occasionally play golf.
**What are your hobbies and interests outside sport?**
I like living the quiet life in Brazil.
**Favourite films?**
I enjoyed watching "The Sixth Sense." But at the moment I prefer to spend my free time with my son, Eduardo.
**Favourite actor?**
Robert de Niro, Cameron Diaz and Robin Williams.
**What do you watch on TV?**
Anything entertaining.
**Favourite music?**
Of course, I have a preference for Brazilian music. But I like most hits, except the heavy stuff.
**Favourite reading matter?**
Sports newspapers.
**What is your favourite holiday destination?**
In Brazil, on the beach, or at home with the family.
**Favourite shopping city?**
Miami, USA.
**Do you have any pets?**
I have three Labradors in Brazil.
**Outside of motorsport, do you admire anyone in particular?**
My family.
**If you were on a desert island, what would you take with you?**
My wife Silvana and my son Eduardo.
**Your ideal day?**
To be in the sunshine with my wife and son and friends.
**What would you do if you were not a racing driver?**
I have never thought of doing anything else.
**What is the most important thing in life?**
To be happy.
**What do you like most about your job?**
The sensation of speed and the pleasure of winning.
**What are your main strengths?**
Originality.
**Have you got any faults?**
I've sometimes not dealt well with pressure.
**Have you thought about your retirement from racing?**
The day I wake up without the desire to win, I'll retire. I live from day to day and don't make long-term plans.

# McLAREN MERCEDES

The years follow one another and nothing seems to change. For the third time in a row, the silver arrows missed the target. Even more so than in 2000, the McLaren-Mercedes were powerless against Ferrari's triumphal progress. With two-thirds of the championship completed, the championship was pretty much over. Ron Dennis, who steers his team with a rod of iron could not stomach this defeat. However, he could not put too much of the blame on his drivers. All year long, Mika Häkkinen was dogged by incredible bad luck. In the end the Finn lost his motivation and decided to take a year off. For his part, David Coulthard proved more consistent than in the past, but he never really posed a threat to Ferrari. There is no doubt he improves with each passing year, but he is still no real match for his main rival, Michael Schumacher. For 2002, he expects to have the full attention of his team, with all the advantages that go with that.

However, backing one driver is not McLaren's style and although commendable in the purely sporting sense, it is clear this is no longer the most efficient way of winning championships. But that's the way it will be and the poor Scotsman better learn to deal with it.

With the arrival of young prodigy, Räikkönen, the McLarens will be serious contenders for victory. If the less than perfect reliability in 2001 can be improved, and if the storm over Adrian Newey almost leaving the team has abated, the silver arrows could shine once more. Tyres have always played a vital role in the final results. In 2001, McLaren did not feel it had the full support of Bridgestone, reckoning it was at a disadvantage compared with Ferrari. So it switched to the enemy camp, welcomed with open arms by Michelin, who did not have to be asked twice.

Ron Dennis cannot stand being beaten. Having snaffled Räikkönen from under Ferrari's nose, he hopes to bring this transitional phase to a speedy conclusion.

Address: McLaren International Ltd
Woking Business Park,
Albert Drive Sheerwater,
Woking, Surrey GU21 5JY,
Great Britain
Tel: +44 (0)1483 711 311
Fax: +44 (0)1483 711 312
Internet: www.mclaren.com

Team principal: Ron Dennis
Technical Director: Adrian Newey
Number of staff: 485

GP debut: Monaco 1966
Number of GP participations: 526
First win: Belgium 1968 (B. McLaren)
Number of wins: 134
Number of pole positions: 112
Number of fastest race laps: 107
Total points scored: 2,583.5
Points average per race: 4.91

Constructors' World titles : 8 (1974, 84, 85, 88, 89, 90, 91 and 98)
Drivers' World titles: 11 (E. Fittipaldi: 1974, Hunt: 1976, Lauda: 1984,
Prost: 1985, 86 and 89, Senna: 1988, 90 and 91, Häkkinen: 1998 and 99)

3rd driver: Alexander Wurz

2001 classification: 2nd (102 points)

- Ron Dennis doesn't like losing!
- Excellent budget.
- Brilliant drivers.
- Mercedes power.
- Very strong technical team.
- Collaboration with Michelin.
- Need for revenge and high motivation.

## The 2001 season summary...

## Weak points

- 2nd in the Constructors' World Championship
- 4 wins (Coulthard 2, Häkkinen 2)
- 2 pole positions (Coulthard 2, Häkkinen 2)
- 6 fastest race laps (Coulthard 3, Häkkinen 3)
- 102 points scored (Coulthard 65, Häkkinen 37)
- 22 Grands Prix finishes from 34 starts (Coulthard 13, Häkkinen 9)
- 22 points-scoring Grand Prix finishes

- No driver hierarchy.
- Rivalry between the drivers.
- Räikkönen's lack of experience.
- Occasional weak race strategy.

Ron *Dennis*    Adrian *Newey*

# DAVID COULTHARD

*McLaren Mercedes*

Last year, David Coulthard was Michael Schumacher's main rival for the title. But it did not take long before he was left behind and had to give best to the German driver. For 2002, the Scotsman hopes he can count on unconditional support from McLaren in his bid for the world championship. The departure of Mika Häkkinen has left him on a mission. An occasional lack of consistency has often caught him out in the past. Maybe, that is the only area where he can improve. He is always brilliant in qualifying, as was seen in Monaco in 2001, when he snatched the pole away from Michael Schumacher. In the races he is a brave and aggressive driver and there is not much lacking in his armoury. Finally out of Mika Häkkinen's shadow and pushed on by the young Kimi Räikkönen, who will not make life easy for him, David Coulthard will be a serious contender for top honours.

Coming back from the long winter break, he was in determined mood, just as he is every year. He knows he can count on Ron Dennis and McLaren to give him the equipment he needs to spoil Ferrari's party.

He is a real gentleman, always smiling and happy to deal with the media, with whom he is in great demand. He is one of the most endearing characters in the sport. Like his friend Jacques Villeneuve, he snubs staying in hotels at the European grands prix, preferring to stay in a luxurious motorhome close to the paddock - which would not look out of place inside it.

For many years now, "DC" has felt he can be champion. Now, as he strolls into the circuit with his beautiful Brazilian girlfriend, Simone, he feels his hour has come.

# David Coulthard

Date and place of birth: March 27, 1971 in Twynholm (Scotland)
Nationality: British
Lives: Monte-Carlo
Marital status: Single
Height: 1,82 m     Weight: 75 kg

Internet: www.davidcoulthard.com

## Career summary

Racing debut: 1983 (karts)
GP debut: Spain 1994 (Williams)

124 Grands Prix
359 points scored
Points average per GP: 2.89
51 podiums
11 wins
24 second places
16 third places
6 fourth places
9 fifth places
5 sixth places
12 pole positions
17 fastest race laps

Qualifying score in 2001: Coulthard 8 / Häkkinen 9

Title:
Formula Ford junior champion in 1989.

## F1 Record

Best classification in F1: 2nd in 2001 (McLaren)
Best GP result: 1st (11 wins)
Best qualification in F1: 1st (12 pole positions)

1994: Williams, 14 points, 8th
1995: Williams, 49 points, 3rd
1996: McLaren, 18 points, 7th
1997: McLaren, 36 points, 3rd
1998: McLaren, 56 points, 3rd
1999: McLaren, 45 points, 4th
2000: McLaren, 73 points, 3rd
2001: McLaren, 65 points, 2nd

F1 team-mates:
1994 and 1995: D. Hill
1996, 1997, 1998, 1999, 2000
and 2001: M. Häkkinen

**First car driven?**
I can't remember what sort of car it was, but I was sitting on my mother's lap at the age of about eight.
**Road car?**
My favourite car is a 1971 Mercedes SEL cabriolet. I also have a Mercedes S 55 AMG and a CL 55 AMG. The Mercedes SL 500 is fantastic, definitely my favourite modern Mercedes-Benz model.
**Favourite or dream car?**
It's still the McLaren F1 Road Car.
**Best race car?**
I'd find it difficult to chose between all the F1 cars I have driven since 1994. Hopefully the West McLaren Mercedes MP4-17.
**Worst race car?**
Without a doubt, it would be the 1990 Vauxhall Lotus.
**Best racing memory?**
My Formula 3 win in Macau in 1991 and the first time I drove an F1 car when I was 19. Also my first F1 win in 1995, and Magny-Cours in 2000.
**Worst racing memory?**
After my win in Magny-Cours, everything went wrong.
**Your racing ambition?**
Becoming an F1 driver was a dream. Now I want to be world champion. It's an obsession I've had since I first started karting.
**Your favourite circuit?**
Spa of course!
**Your least favourite circuit?**
I still don't like Budapest.
**Your favourite driver of all time?**
Clark, Prost, Mansell and Senna.
**Your favourite driver of the current batch?**
Jacques Villeneuve is a good mate.
**Favourite dish?**
Pasta.
**Favourite drink?**
Tea and mineral water.
**Sports you participate in?**
Golf, jogging, gym, cycling and swimming.
**Favourite sport?**
I like athletics.
**Favourite sports star?**
The athlete Linford Christie and motorcycle racer Mika Doohan, because I admire his courage.
**What are your hobbies and interests outside sport?**
I like to feel free, I love the water and being on a boat, spending time with friends and watching films.
**Favourite films?**
I love the cinema. Over the grand prix weekends in Europe, I live in the motorhome. I have a television fitted with a giant screen to see all my favourite films. "Lord of the rings", I enjoyed the books when I was younger and the film met my expectations.

**Favourite actor?**
Tom Cruise and Harrison Ford.
**What do you watch on TV?**
I don't watch television.
**Favourite music?**
All pop music: Madonna, Robbie Williams, the Cranberries, the Corrs and Oasis. I keep hearing rumours that Oasis are working on a new album and I'm very much looking forward to hearing that.
**Favourite reading matter?**
I don't read much.
**What is your favourite holiday destination?**
Somewhere I can be on a boat.
**Favourite shopping city?**
London, Milan, Paris and New York.
**Do you have any pets?**
A small dog.
**Outside of motorsport, do you admire anyone in particular?**
Linford Christie for his fantastic 100 metres and Sean Connery, playing the part of James Bond.
**If you were on a desert island, what would you take with you?**
I would not go on my own.
**Your ideal day?**
To start with, there would be no alarm call. Then, some time in the gym, a trip on a boat with my friends, have a drink, take a nap and relax somewhere like Saint-Tropez.
**What would you do if you were not a racing driver?**
My parents run a transport business. I would like to have worked in the music business.
**What is the most important thing in life?**
Health.
**What do you like most about your job?**
The sense of speed.
**What are your main strengths?**
You would have to ask someone else.
**Have you got any faults?**
I've got too many!
**Have you thought about your retirement from racing?**
I would like to stay in the business. Maybe I could be a journalist to criticise the others.

# KIMI **RÄIKKÖNEN**
## *McLaren Mercedes*

At the tender age of 11, Kimi Räikkönen had his first go at karting. Ten years later, he competed in his first car race. He had a short apprenticeship, and soon became a regular on the podium in the British Formula Renault series, which he won easily in 2000. In the autumn of that year, Peter Sauber invited the young unknown to try a few laps in one his cars, at Mugello. Impressed, he decided to sign him up for the 2001 season. The FIA gave him the Superlicense required to race in Formula 1, but Max Mosley and several drivers expressed their doubts. However, having followed him for a few laps in testing, Michael Schumacher no less sprung to Räikkönen's defense. The four-times world champion certainly had no idea that the Finn could well pose a serious threat to him just one year later.

Courted by Ferrari, it was McLaren which finally seduced the young man from the frozen North. He is an enigmatic character and seems immune to pressure. He is impressive, given that he appears calm, mature and determined.

Ron Dennis finds it hard to hide his delight in having enrolled the young lad with the ice blue eyes. He is convinced he will win grands prix this year. After Keke Rosberg and Mika Häkkinen, it seems that Kimi Räikkönen is destined to be the next Flying Finn. Right from his first test in a McLaren in January, the young prodigy, who is scared of nothing and of no one, was capable of matching Coulthard's times. Hardly out of adolescence, this strange and mysterious character knows he will be one of the key players this year.

After an amazing debut year with Williams, Jenson Button suffered badly at Benetton last season. Could the same thing happen to Kimi Räikkönen? McLaren can be counted on to get the best out of him.

## Kimi Räikkönen

Date and place of birth: October 17, 1979 in Espoo (Finland)
Nationality: Finnish
Lives: Espoo (Finland) and Chigwell (Great Britain)
Marital status: Single
Height: 1,75 m    Weight: 62 kg

Internet: www.kimiraikkonen.com

### Career summary

Racing debut: 1990 (karts)
GP debut: Australia 2001 (Sauber)

17 Grands Prix
9 points scored
Points average per GP: 0.52
0 podiums
0 wins
2 fourth places
1 fifth place
1 sixth place

Qualifying score in 2001: Räikkönen 7 / Heidfeld 10

Titles:
Winner of the British Formula Renault winter series in 1999.
British Formula Renault champion in 2000.

### F1 Record

Best classification in F1: 10th in 2001 (Sauber)
Best GP result: 4th (Austria and Canada 2001)
Best qualification in F1: 7th (Canada and Great Britain 2001)

2001: Sauber, 9 points, 10th

F1 team-mate:
2001: N. Heidfeld

**First car driven?**
A Lada, in Finland.
**Road car?**
A Mercedes C 32 AMG in Finland, and a Mercedes ML 270 CDI in Switzerland.
**Favourite or dream car?**
Lamborghinis and the Ferrari Modena.
**Best race car?**
Driving a McLaren is a dream come true.
**Worst race car?**
Formula Ford.
**Best racing memory?**
My fourth place in Canada with Sauber in 2001 is my best result to date. But the first time I drove a McLaren was a fantastic moment. The dream had come true.
**Worst racing memory?**
My accident in Suzuka last year.
**Your racing ambition?**
I wanted to be a Formula 1 driver and now I want to win races.
**Your favourite circuit?**
It's hard to say in terms of F1 circuits. I like Donington and Spa.
**Your least favourite circuit?**
I like all the circuits.
**Your favourite driver of all time?**
Ayrton Senna.
**Your favourite driver of the current batch?**
None in particular.
**Favourite dish?**
Pasta with mushroom sauce, chicken dishes and a typical Finnish game dish.
**Favourite drink?**
Pineapple juice, water and milk.
**Sports you participate in?**
Snowboarding, skateboarding, cross-country skiing, ice hockey and jogging.
**Favourite sport?**
The ones I do and all motorised sports.
**Favourite sports star?**
No one in particular.
**What are your hobbies and interests outside sport?**
I like racing too much.
**Favourite films?**
Action films.

**Favourite actor?**
Tom Cruise.
**What sport do you watch on TV?**
Motor sports.
**Favourite music?**
U2, and a Finnish group called Darude.
**Favourite reading matter?**
Autosport and other motoring magazines.
**What is your favourite holiday destination?**
Sunny beaches of Lapland, where I can go snowboarding.
**Favourite shopping city?**
I never used to like shopping for clothes. Since I visited Hugo Boss in Germany, that's changed.
**Do you have any pets?**
Sadly no, because I travel too much.
**Outside of motorsport, do you admire anyone in particular?**
Not really.
**If you were on a desert island, what would you take with you?**
My girlfriend Hanna, a television and a racing car.
**Your ideal day?**
It would start with snowboarding in Lapland.
**What would you do if you were not a racing driver?**
(laughs)
**What is the most important thing in life?**
To realise your dreams.
**What do you like most about your job?**
Winning.
**What are your main strengths?**
You'll have to ask my mother!
**Have you got any faults?**
Like everyone, I am too clever.
**Have you thought about your retirement from racing?**
Not yet. I could imagine lying on a sunny beach. I could get a tan without any bother and then alternate that with skiing for hours.

# WILLIAMSBMW

As pragmatic as ever, Sir Frank Williams stated his clear objectives for 2002: "We want to and we must be in the fight for the title. We have the strongest driver pairing. Ralf Schumacher and Juan Pablo Montoya are different, both in terms of personality and driving style. But they have the same aim: to win." The four victories obtained last year by the blue and white cars were just a step in Williams-BMW's ambitious programme. Returning to Formula 1, the Munich marque was not back to make up the numbers, while in Williams, it had a partner which felt that five years since its last title was way too long.

The engine power on offer from BMW is now very impressive. Rumour has it that the new P82 engine kicks out around 900 bhp. We are gradually getting close to the power output of the turbo engines in the Eighties. The amount of money invested in Formula 1 is increasing at a monstrous pace. In these days of recession, Williams has still managed to pull in two new sponsors, FedEx and 7 Up. Close cooperation with Michelin, despite the arrival of McLaren, has already born fruit.

The Williams FW24 is not a revolutionary car. It is an evolution of the previous model. Main changes are on the aerodynamic front to make the car more efficient on all types of track. The drivers are not the best of friends and Frank Williams delights in the tension this creates. It will only serve to make his team more competitive. The team knows how to deal with conflict of this sort, having seen it all before with the Jones-Reutemann, Rosberg-Mansell and Piquet-Mansell duos in the past.

Ralf Schumacher and Juan Pablo Montoya never speak to one another, aside from the technical briefings, and conviviality is not the order of the day in this team. Efficiency is what matters. Having rediscovered the taste of victory, Williams does not want to leave it at that. It wants to mix it with Ferrari and McLaren for overall honours.

## BMW.WilliamsF1 Team

Address: BMW Williams F1
Grove, Wantage, Oxfordshire
OX12 ODQ, Great Britain
Tel: +44 (0)1235 77 77 00
Fax: +44 (0)1235 76 47 05
Internet: www.bmw.williamsf1.com

Team principal: Frank Williams
Technical Director: Patrick Head
Number of staff: 400

GP debut: Argentina 1978
Number of GP participations: 428
First win: Great Britain 1979 (C. Regazzoni)
Number of wins: 103
Number of pole positions: 108
Number of fastest race laps: 110
Total points scored: 2,031.5
Points average per race: 4.74

Constructors' world titles: 9 (1980, 81,86, 87, 92, 93, 94, 96 and 97)
Drivers' world titles: 7 (Jones: 1980, Rosberg: 1982, Piquet: 1986, Mansell: 1992, Prost: 1993, D. Hill: 1996, J. Villeneuve: 1997)

3rd driver: Marc Gené (Spain)

Test driver: Antonio Pizzonia (Brazil)

2001 classification: 3rd (80 points )

### Strong points

- Very good budget.
- Excellent driver pairing.
- Their rivalry can push the team forward.
- BMW technology and resources.
- Very strong technical team.
- Enormous motivation.

### The 2001 season summary...

- 3rd in the Constructors' World Championship
- 4 wins (R. Schumacher 3, Montoya 1)
- 4 pole positions (Montoya 3, R. Schumacher 1)
- 8 fastest race laps (R. Schumacher 5, Montoya 3)
- 80 points scored (R. Schumacher 49, Montoya 31)
- 14 Grands Prix finishes from 34 starts (R. Schumacher 9, Montoya 5)
- 14 points-scoring Grand Prix finishes

### Weak points

- Too much rivalry between the drivers.
- Williams is no longer the only top team on Michelin tyres.
- Loss of aerodynamicist Geoff Willis to BAR.
- Race strategy sometimes weak.

Frank Williams   Patrick Head

# RALF**SCHUMACHER**

*Williams BMW*

5

When he started in Formula 1, the younger of the Schumacher brothers paraded his arrogance through the paddock. He appeared haughty, disdainful and seemed to think he came from divine dynasty. But a few good slaps in the face from Jordan team-mate Giancarlo Fisichella began to get his ideas straightened out. The man who was just known as "the brother" gradually became more accessible, more down to earth. He married the beautiful Cora who presented him with a son, David. Like a good wine, he has improved with age. He has finally emerged from his brother's shadow to become his own man. He has a first name now and has no need to envy anyone. He faced a new hurdle at Williams in 2001, in the shape of the diabolical Montoya, winning three grands prix and enjoying an excellent season. As he said last year: "If I am not quicker than Montoya, I might as well go and do something else."

But he has to be on his guard. Towards the end of last year, the Colombian began to have a slight edge over him. He found it hard to stomach and is evidently a bad loser, but he will not accept defeat. Last year in parc ferme at Monza, he refused to salute his team-mate, who had just won the race. Ralf Schumacher is well aware of Montoya's ability.

Williams are used to dealing with the big personalities and this rivalry is something Frank Williams appreciates, feeling it adds a competitive edge to his team.

Ralf does not hide the fact. "I wouldn't say he was my best friend, but our professional relationship is fine." Like his brother Michael at Ferrari, he has extended his contract to the end of 2004. With that matter out of the way, he will be able to concentrate full time on getting ahead of, containing and mastering Juan Pablo Montoya, his "bete noir". If he manages it, he will be able to stand comparison with his brother.

# Ralf Schumacher

Date and place of birth: June 30, 1975 in Hurth-Hermühlheim (Germany)
Nationality: German
Lives: Monte Carlo
Marital status: Married to Cora, one child (David)
Height: 1,78 m     Weight: 73 kg

Internet: www.ralf-schumacher.net

## Career summary

Racing debut: 1974 (karts)
GP debut: Australia 1997 (Jordan)

83 Grands Prix
135 points scored
Points average per GP: 1.62
14 podiums
3 wins
3 second places
8 third places
9 fourth places
12 fifth places
4 sixth places
1 pole position
6 fastest race laps

Qualifying score in 2001: Schumacher 11 / Montoya 6

Titles:
Winner of the Formula 3 Macao Grand Prix in 1995.
Japanese F3000 champion in 1996.

## F1 Record

Best classification in F1: 4th in 2001 (Williams)
Best GP result:1st (3 wins)
Best qualification in F1: 1st (France 2001)

1997: Jordan, 13 points, 11th
1998: Jordan, 14 points, 10th
1999: Williams, 35 points, 6th
2000: Williams, 24 points, 5th
2001: Williams, 49 points, 4th

F1 team-mates:
1997: G. Fisichella
1998: D.Hill
1999: A. Zanardi
2000: J. Button
2001: J.P. Montoya

**First car driven?**
A Fiat 500 when I was 7.
**Road car?**
A BMW M5 and an X5.
**Favourite or dream car?**
None really.
**Best race car?**
The 2001 Williams FW 23 and the 1998 Jordan.
**Worst race car?**
It wouldn't be nice to complain for the people who entrusted me with it.
**Best racing memory?**
My three wins last year are great memories. I also enjoyed finding myself on the podium with my brother in Montreal.
**Worst racing memory?**
I always try and forget these things very quickly.
**Your racing ambition?**
I have a long-term contract with BMW. It's an excellent challenge.
**Your favourite circuit?**
Monaco.
**Your least favourite circuit?**
None in particular.
**Your favourite driver of all time?**
None.

**Your favourite driver of the current batch?**
My brother Michael, of course.
**Favourite dish?**
Pasta.
**Favourite drink?**
Apple juice with sparkling water.
**Sports you participate in?**
Tennis, cycling, karting and training.
**Favourite sport?**
The Olympic Games, basketball and athletics.
**Favourite sports star?**
Top sports stars in general.
**What are your hobbies and interests outside sport?**
I love playing backgammon.
**Favourite films?**
Action films and comedies. Since I got married and my son David was born, I have not had time to go to the cinema.
**Favourite actor?**
Bill Cosby.
**What do you watch on TV?**
I sometimes watch it just to have a break.
**Favourite music?**
Soft rock.
**Favourite reading matter?**
I don't read much.
**What is your favourite holiday destination?**
My home in Monte Carlo.
**Favourite shopping city?**
Singapore.
**Do you have any pets?**
A dog.
**Outside of motorsport, do you admire anyone in particular?**
My brother and my family.
**If you were on a desert island, what would you take with you?**
A boat to get off the island as quickly as possible.
**Your ideal day?**
Being at home, looking after my son and relaxing.
**What would you do if you were not a racing driver?**
I think I would have been a businessman.
**What is the most important thing in life?**
Health, earning a good living and reaching the objectives you have set yourself.
**What do you like most about your job?**
Driving.
**What are your main strengths?**
I am very strong mentally.
**Have you got any faults?**
I am too selfish.
**Have you thought about your retirement from racing?**
For the moment, I haven't thought about it.

# JUAN PABLO MONTOYA  6

## Williams BMW

In 1997, Frank Williams had already spotted the young Columbian flyer, who was sparkling in F3000. "This guy is something special!"

He did not waste time and signed him as a test driver the next year. But there was no room in his driver line-up and Williams let him go to the United States, guaranteeing him a drive in 2001.

Juan Pablo Montoya was an aggressive success across the Pond. In his first year, he won the Cart championship and the Indy 500 the following season. Back home, he made his Formula 1 debut for Williams last year, just as the team was coming good after a difficult patch. In Brazil, right from the third race of the season, the little Colombian went head to head with the fortress Michael Schumacher. In the Senna Esses, he pulled off a remarkable move. Neither driver would give ground and they raced wheel to wheel for fifty metres, before the world champion was forced to lift off. It was the defining moment and proof that here was another champion in the making. This duel was compared to the famous battle between Villeneuve and Arnoux at Dijon in 1979. Later, his lack of experience sometimes he caught him out, despite his talent for attacking. He tried a bit too hard on the track. Arrogant and insolent, he also found it difficult to match team-mate Ralf Schumacher, who became his main opposition.

The two men do not get on and loathe one another in polite fashion. After almost coming to blows with Jacques Villeneuve in Montreal, Montoya took the wise decision to calm down, after called to order by Frank Williams. And then, as if by magic, the results started to come. He took three pole positions in the second half of the season and won in fine style at Monza.

The Colombian flags now fly in all four corners of the globe and his fans are ever more numerous, while he has rapidly become a major Formula 1 star.

It is likely that this little man with the raucous laugh will give the Schumacher brothers a hard time this year.

# Juan Pablo Montoya

Date and place of birth: September 20, 1975 in Bogota (Colombia)
Nationality: Colombian
Lives: Monte-Carlo, Oxford and Madrid
Marital status: Engaged to Connie
Height: 1,68 m    Weight: 72 kg

Internet: www.jpmontoya.com

## Career summary

Racing debut: 1981 (karts)
GP debut: Australia 2001 (Williams)

17 Grands Prix
31 points scored
Points average per GP: 1.82
1 win (Italy 2001)
3 second places
1 fourth place
3 pole positions
3 fastest race laps

Qualifying score in 2001: Montoya 6 / Schumacher 11

Titles:
Two-times World Junior karting champion in 1991 and 1992.
International F3000 champion in 1998.
CART champion in 1999.
Winner of the Indianapolis 500 Miles in 2000.

## F1 Record

Best classification in F1: 6th in 2001 (Williams)
Best GP result: 1st (Italy 2001)
Best qualification in F1:
1st (Germany, Belgium and Italy 2001)

2001: Williams, 31 points, 6th

F1 team-mate:
2001: R. Schumacher

**First car driven?**
My father's car, when I was 14.
**Road car?**
A BMW M5.
**Favourite car or dream car?**
I would like to have driven Graham Hill's Lotus 49. It must have been a beast to drive.
**Best race car?**
The Williams FW19 that I drove as a test driver in 1998.
**Worst race car?**
No comment.
**Best racing memory?**
Winning the Cart championship in 1999, especially the race at Long Beach and the Indy 500 in 2000.
**Worst racing memory?**
The Mid Ohio race in 2000.
**Your racing ambition?**
That's simple: to win.
**Your favourite circuit?**
I don't have a particular favourite.
**Your least favourite circuit?**
I don't like Barcelona. It's not enjoyable to drive.

**Your favourite driver of all time?**
I admired Ayrton Senna.
**Your favourite driver of the current batch?**
I don't know any of them.
**Favourite dish?**
Pasta.
**Favourite drink?**
Orange juice.
**Sports you participate in?**
Squash, jogging, cycling, water skiing and all water sports.
**Favourite sport?**
Anything with an engine.
**Favourite sports star?**
I don't have one.
**What are your hobbies and interests outside sport?**
Computers and video games.
**Favourite films?**
Action films and comedies.
**Favourite actor?**
Andy McDowell.
**What do you watch on TV?**
I don't like television.
**Favourite music?**
I like rock music, but no one band in particular.
**Favourite reading matter?**
Motorsport magazines.
**What is your favourite holiday destination?**
The Caribbean, but not on my own.
**Favourite shopping city?**
Miami.
**Do you have any pets?**
No, I hate cats and dogs.
**Outside of motorsport, do you admire anyone in particular?**
Some sports stars.
**If you were on a desert island, what would you take with you?**
My girlfriend.
**Your ideal day?**
To be with my family and girlfriend. I like to relax, to chill out and play on the Playstation.
**What would you do if you were not a racing driver?**
I don't know.
**What is the most important thing in life?**
To be respected by others.
**What do you like most about your job?**
Everything about it is a permanent challenge.
**What are your main strengths?**
I am persistent.
**Have you got any faults?**
I don't know.
**Have you thought about your retirement from racing?**
The idea hasn't even crossed my mind.

# SAUBER**PETRONAS**

In 2002, Peter Sauber will celebrate ten years in Formula 1. Against high tides and storms, he has steered his team from splendid isolation in Switzerland with great merit. Last year, Sauber did remarkably well, resulting in an excellent fourth place in the world championship. That was partly due to a complete rethink in terms of his choice of drivers. In the past, the Swiss team had filled its seats with experienced men. But last year, there was a radical change of policy. After the young unknown Finn, Kimi Räikkönen showed promising talent in testing his car, Sauber decided to take him on, despite a general air of scepticism from other teams and the governing body. Alongside him, Nick Heidfeld seemed like a veteran, with 17 Grands Prix under his belt. With this baby line-up, Sauber set the sport alight. But Räikkönen could not resist the siren call of McLaren and the team decided to continue with its youth policy, giving his drive to Felipe Massa, a twenty-year-old Brazilian. While Sauber can be criticised for an old fashioned attitude, this almost invisible squad does not lack ambition. Red Bull has sold off some of its shares in the team, but that does not seem to have made waves, as one would expect with this team. The Sauber C21 looks pretty much like its predecessor, but it is extensively modified. It is still powered by the same Ferrari engine as in 2001, rebadged as Petronas and that will mean good reliability.

Peter Sauber knows just how difficult it will be to hang onto that fourth place. It is an exceptional performance, given that he finished ahead of teams which could count on backing from major car makers such as Ford, Honda and Renault. "We know we are aiming high, but we accept the challenge…" he adds with a wicked grin.

Address: Sauber Motorsport AG
Wildbachstrasse 9, 8340 Hinwil,
Switzerland
Tel: +41 (0)1 937 90 00
Fax: +41 (0)1 937 90 01
Internet: www.sauber-petronas.com

Team principal: Peter Sauber
Technical Director: Willy Rampf
Number of staff: 260

GP debut: South Africa 1993
Number of GP participations: 146
0 wins
0 pole positions
0 fastest race laps
Total points scored: 111
Points average per race: 0.76

Best classification in the Constructors' World Championship: 4th in 2001
Best classification in the Drivers' World Championship: N. Heidfeld, 7th in 2001

3rd driver: none

Test driver: none

2001 classification: 4th (21 points)

- A good budget.
- Excellent 2001 results.
- Talented young drivers.
- Desire to hold station in the rankings.
- Good technical team.
- Strong support from Bridgestone.
- Ferrari engine.

*The 2001 season summary...*

*Weak points*

- 4th in the Constructors' World Championship
- Best result: 3rd (Heidfeld)
- Best qualification: 6th (Heidfeld)
- 21 points scored (Heidfeld 12, Räikkönen 9)
- 21 Grands Prix finishes from 34 starts (Heidfeld 11, Räikkönen 10)
- 11 points-scoring Grand Prix finishes (Heidfeld 7, Räikkönen 4)

- Felipe Massa is a rookie.
- Isolation in Switzerland.
- No support from a major manufacturer.

*Peter Sauber* *Willy Rampf*

# NICK HEIDFELD

*Sauber Petronas*

7

Last year, during a press conference in Monza, Mika Häkkinen announced his intention to take a year's sabbatical from racing. Shortly afterwards, a McLaren press release brought the news that Kimi Räikkönen would be David Coulthard's team-mate in 2002. The news was a firm slap in the face for Nick Heidfeld. Throughout his young career, he had been supported by Mercedes. At the young age of 19, he was already a McLaren test driver. He drove around 10,000 kilometres for the team and built a good base for a career.

In 2000, he did his schooling at Prost Grand Prix, before continuing his apprenticeship with Sauber. It seemed more than likely that, when a seat became available at McLaren, it would fall to Nick Heidfeld, the family son. So it must have been a real shock to hear the name of his own team-mate announced!

It was a bitter pill to swallow. All through 2001, despite some excellent results for the neophyte Räikkönen, the German driver had proved to be dominant in all areas, generally quicker and getting better results. How does one explain this strange decision?

In Formula 1, nothing is impossible. Despite great disappointment, Nick Heidfeld responded with dignity. He remained silent, rather than air his complaints in public. He will therefore continue his career with the pleasant Swiss team, in the hope his star will finally shine.

He has notched up some excellent results and he is definitely one of the best drivers of his generation. He has all the qualities needed to be a true champion.

## Nick Heidfeld

Date and place of birth: May 10, 1977 in Mönchengladbach (Germany)
Nationality: German
Lives: Monte-Carlo
Marital status: Engaged to Patricia
Height: 1,60 m     Weight: 69 kg

Internet: www.nick-heidfeld.com

### Career summary

Racing debut: 1986 (karts)
GP debut: Australia 2000 (Prost)

33 Grands Prix
12 points
0 wins
1 third place
1 fourth place
5 sixth places
0 pole positions
0 fastest race laps

Qualifying score in 2001: Heidfeld 10 / Räikkönen 7

Titles:
German Formula Ford 1600 champion in 1994.
German Formula Ford 1800 champion in 1995.
Winner of the Formula 3 Macao Grand Prix in 1996.
German Formula 3 champion in 1997.
International F3000 champion in 1999.

### F1 Record

Best classification in F1: 7th in 2001 (Sauber)
Best GP result: 3rd (Brazil 2001)
Best qualification in F1: 6th (Austria, GB and USA 2001)

2000: Prost, 0 points, not classified
2001: Sauber, 12 points, 7th

F1 team-mates:
2000: J. Alesi
2001: K. Räikkönen

**First car driven?**
I was sitting on my father's lap in a car park at the Nürburgring. I was not quite ten years old, but I really can't remember what the car was.

**Road car?**
A Toyota Lexus GRX 300

**Favourite or dream car?**
There are a lot I like, but I don't dream about them.

**Best race car?**
The F3 Dallara at the Nürburgring in 1997, and my F3000 at Imola in 1999.

**Worst race car?**
The Prost AP03 in 2000.

**Best racing memory?**
My first podium in F1 in Brazil last year.

**Worst racing memory?**
The Nürburgring in 2000, when I qualified well in the Prost, only to retire very early in the race.

**Your racing ambition?**
To be happy with what I do. For the moment that means racing, but in the future, it might be something else.

**Your favourite circuit?**
Street circuits like Macau and Monaco, and then the Nürburgring.

**Your least favourite circuit?**
I don't like Spa nor tracks on airfields.

**Your favourite driver of all time?**
Ayrton Senna and Alain Prost

**Your favourite driver of the current batch?**
None really.

**Favourite dish?**
Italian cuisine and subtle buffet starters.

**Favourite drink?**
Orange juice with sparkling water.

**Sports you participate in?**
I love tennis, but I don't get much time to play. Golf, working in the gym, beach volley ball and road cycling.

**Favourite sport?**
I'm interested in all sports.

**Favourite sports star?**
The basketball player Michael Jordan. His comeback has impressed me.

**What are your hobbies and interests outside sport?**
I need to play sports. Apart from that, I like motorcycling. I started when I was five, but it's too dangerous. I also like the cinema and music.

**Favourite films?**
I like the Fifth Element, Pulp Fiction and Lord of the Rings.

**Favourite actor?**
Cameron Diaz.

**What sport do you watch on TV?**
Motorised sports and major soccer and boxing events.

**Favourite music?**
I like pop stuff in the charts and especially the American band, Outkast, Miss Jackson, Moby, Texas, Lauren Hill, Wutang Clan, Alcazar and Kylie Minogue.

**Favourite reading matter?**
Car magazines.

**What is your favourite holiday destination?**
I would like to go to Australia more often. Unfortunately it's a bit far... I really like Perth, Sydney, and I would like to visit Queensland.

**Favourite shopping city?**
I have no favourites. Sydney's nice but a bit far away.

**Do you have any pets?**
I like animals. Sadly, my father is allergic to them so we never had any and now, I am never at home.

**Outside of motorsport, do you admire anyone in particular?**
No, not really.

**If you went to a desert island, what would you take with you?**
My girlfriend Patricia, thousands of bottles of Coca-Cola and a genius to get me off the island.

**Your ideal day?**
To be on a sunny island with my girlfriend Patricia, my family and friends. I would relax, do a bit of sport, surf, beach volley-ball and spend an enjoyable time. In the evening, I would have a barbecue and drink a couple of beers.

**What would you do if you were not a racing driver?**
I would certainly have done another sport. I like the spirit of competition.

**What is the most important thing in life?**
To be happy.

**What do you like most about your job?**
Driving.

**What are your main strengths?**
I am realistic and can analyse things.

**Have you got any faults?**
Like everyone, I have a lot.

**Have you thought about your retirement from racing?**
No, not yet.

# FELIPE MASSA

*Sauber Petronas*

The 2000 European Formula Renault series went down to a duel between two promising young drivers at Valencia, Spain. Taking the upper hand was Felipe Massa, a 19-year old Brazilian, who just got the better of Kimi Räikkönen, a 20-year old Finn. These two youngsters could hardly imagine that they would be in Formula 1 eighteen months later, thanks to Peter Sauber, who seems to be an expert talent spotter. From an average Sao Paulo family, Felipe Massa made the obligatory debut in karting, before moving to Italy with a rather meagre budget. Despite that, he picked up a drive with a good Formula Renault team and made the most of it. Last year, in the Italian F3000 series, he continued his meteoric climb. Ferrari thought about taking him on as a test driver and recommended him highly to Peter Sauber, who had just lost Räikkönen to McLaren. It was a case of cause and effect, and after an impressive test session in Mugello, Felipe Massa was hired by the Swiss team.

The Italian press were quick to dub Massa the new Senna. Physically, he looks more like Nelson Piquet, with whom he seems to share a relaxed approach to life. He is straightforward and easygoing, and the team is already convinced of his abilities. He hopes to emulate Räikkönen at Sauber, even if they are poles apart. One is blonde and shy, the other is tanned and outgoing. The only thing they have in common is their age and prodigious talent. They both come from the baby category, are scared of nothing and brim with the confidence that they can get the job done.

The latest prodigy to come out of Brazil seems to have a bright future ahead of him. In fact, his favourite drink is champagne, best drunk on the podium, a place he is particularly keen on.

## Felipe Massa

Date and place of birth: April 25, 1981 in Sao Paolo (Brazil)
Nationality: Brazilian
Lives: Hinwil (Switzerland)
Marital status: Single
Height: 1,67 m    Weight: 59 kg

Internet: www.felipemassa.com

## Career summary

Racing debut: 1990 (karts)
GP debut: Australia 2002 (Sauber)

Titles:
Brazilian Formula Chevrolet-Opel champion in 1999.
European and Italian Formula Renault champion in 2000.
Italian Euro 3000 champion in 2001.

**First car driven?**
I was about 8 or 9, but I can't remember what make of car I was giving a hard time!
**Road car?**
A Lexus 4x4.
**Favourite or dream car?**
The Ferrari Maranello.
**Best race car?**
The Sauber and my F3000.
**Worst race car?**
The Formula Chevrolet-Opel.
**Best racing memory?**
When I won the European title in Formula Renault at Valencia in 2000, and last year's victory in the Euro 3000 at the Nürburgring.
**Worst racing memory?**
It was at Varano in Formula Renault. I was out on my own in the lead and I spun off.
**Your racing ambition?**
To be F1 world champion.
**Your favourite circuit?**
Fast circuits like Spa and Mugello.
**Your least favourite circuit?**
I don't like Varano, which is too tight.
**Your favourite driver of all time?**
I was 13 when Senna was killed at Imola. I was a bit too young to follow his feats. I also liked Piquet.
**Your favourite driver of the current batch?**
I am impressed by Michael Schumacher.
**Favourite dish?**
All sorts of pasta and meat, and Brazilian dishes.
**Favourite drink?**
Champagne on the podium.
**Sports you participate in?**
Jogging, cycling, swimming, weight training and tennis.
**Favourite sport?**
Football, water skiing and jet ski.
**Favourite sports star?**
The tennis player Gustavo Kuerten and footballers Ronaldo and Romario.
**What are your hobbies and interests outside sport?**
Going out with mates, meeting people, talking, listening to music and going to the cinema.

**Favourite films?**
I like Casino and any suspense films.
**Favourite actor?**
I love Robert de Niro and Bruce Willis.
**What sport do you watch on TV?**
I used to watch the grands prix. Now I will be taking part in them. I also like watching comedy shows.
**Favourite music?**
I like all sorts of music, from hip-hop to dance music and techno.
**Favourite reading matter?**
Car and news magazines.
**What is your favourite holiday destination?**
Brazil of course! I like going to Angra dos Reis and Isola Bella.
**Favourite shopping city?**
Big cities like London, Paris, Milan and Sao Paulo.
**Do you have any pets?**
Two labradors back in Brazil.
**Outside of motorsport, do you admire anyone in particular?**
My family.
**If you were on a desert island, what would you take with you?**
A girl and a pistol to blow my brains out if I have no way of escaping.
**Your ideal day?**
Being on holiday.
**What would you do if you were not a racing driver?**
I haven't got a clue.
**What is the most important thing in life?**
Racing and my family.
**What do you like most about your job?**
The feeling of speed and the adrenalin.
**What are your main strengths?**
I have a happy disposition. I like talking to people and I reckon I'm easy to get along with.
**Have you got any faults?**
Loads.
**Have you thought about your retirement from racing?**
I would switch to other categories after F1.

# JORDAN HONDA

In continuing his seduction of Honda, wily old Eddie Jordan had no hesitation in serving notice to his friend Jean Alesi, to make way for his engine supplier's favourite son, Takuma Sato. Times are hard. The mysterious sacking of Heinz-Harald Frentzen after the British Grand Prix had strained relations with some of the sponsors, like cigarette brand Benson & Hedges and negotiations with partners were getting difficult. When it ran it Spain, the new car was in a plain yellow livery, which is not the usual Jordan way, given that in the past, their cars looked like Christmas trees. Giancarlo Fisichella returns to this team after a long stay at Benetton. He and Jarno Trulli have swopped seats.

The little Italian hopes to get back on top. He is at a key point in his career. He has all the necessary qualities to drag this team out of the doldrums. Last year, the yellow cars were quick but fragile. Competing against the similarly powered BARs, good results are now essential. Honda will soon have to chose and drop one of its customers.

The manufacturers are not beating a path to Jordan's door. It is a matter of survival and Eddie Jordan understands that better than anyone. This year, the absence of change to the technical regulations has prompted many teams to adopt a conservative approach, with minor changes rather than radical re-designs. However, the Jordan-Honda EJ12 sports a daring and innovative aerodynamic package.

Will this risk-taking be rewarded with success? The survival of this young and dynamic team, which has often provided some colour in a sport suffering the odd bout of torpor and lethargy, may well depend on it.

## Strong points

Address: Jordan Grand Prix Ltd
Silverstone, Northants
NN 12 8TJ, Great Britain
Tel: +44 (0)1327 85 08 00
Fax: +44 (0)1327 85 79 93
Internet: www.jordangp.com

Team principal: Eddie Jordan
Technical Director: Eghbal Hamidy
Number of staff: 220

GP debut: United States 1991
Number of GP participations: 180
First win: Belgium 1998 (D. Hill)
Number of wins: 3
Number of pole positions: 2
Number of fastest race laps: 2
Total points scored: 252
Points average per race: 1.4

Best classification in the Constructors' World Championship: 3rd in 1999
Best classification in the Drivers' World Championship: H.-H. Frentzen, 3rd in 1999

3rd driver: none

Test driver: none

2001 classification: 5th (19 points)

- The arrival of Giancarlo Fisichella.
- Support from Honda.
- The presence of Takuma Sato, a Honda driver.
- The desire to start afresh.
- Can be directly compared with BAR.

## The 2001 season summary...

- 5th in the Constructors' World Championship
- Best result: 4th (Trulli)
- Best qualification: 4th (Trulli)
- 19 points scored (Trulli 12, Frentzen 6, Alesi 1)
- 18 Grands Prix finishes from 34 starts (Trulli 8, Frentzen 6, Alesi 4)
- 8 points-scoring Grand Prix finishes (Trulli 5, Frentzen 3, Alesi 1)
- 4 drivers entered (Trulli 17 GP, Frentzen 10, Zonta 2 and Alesi 5)

## Weak points

- Financial difficulties.
- Will the new car be reliable?
- Sato's lack of experience.
- The team needs to find its second wind.
- The team must deliver.

*Eddie Jordan* *Eghbal Hamidy*

# GIANCARLOFISICHELLA

*9*

*Jordan Honda*

Giancarlo Fisichella spent four years with Benetton. Flavio Briatore wanted to team him up with Jarno Trulli in the new Renault team. But Jenson Button, despite a difficult year, stayed put thanks to a cast iron contract. So the little Roman had to move on. He found a berth at Jordan, the team with which he competed in his first full season of Formula 1, in 1997. It is therefore a case of going back to his roots. Despite backing from Honda, Jordan is reckoned to be in financial difficulties. One of the clauses in his three-year contract allows Fisichella to move on if the car does not live up to his expectations.

In 2001, not many people fancied Fisico's chances against the Button tornado. The opposite was true. The Italian driver dominated his team-mate in every respect. He emerged with honours from what was a running-in year for the future Renault team. His third place in Spa, after a brilliant drive, meant that Benetton saved face and regained some dignity after a very tough season.

Giancarlo Fisichella does not have a track record worthy of his ability. He is a charming lad, ever smiling and available and is in every way, a top driver. He has always had the upper hand over his team-mates, as was the case with Ralf Schumacher at Jordan in 1997. He has come close to winning on several occasions, finishing second five times, while qualifying brilliantly. If Eddie Jordan can give him the right equipment, the Italian will know how to get the best out of it.

# Giancarlo Fisichella

Date and place of birth: January 14, 1973 in Rome (Italy)
Nationality: Italian
Lives: Monte Carlo
Marital status: Married to Luna, one daughter Carlotta
Height: 1,72 m     Weight: 69 kg

Internet: www.giancarlofisichella.com

## Career summary

Racing debut: 1984 (karts)
GP debut: Australia 1996 (Minardi)

91 Grands Prix
75 points scored
Points average per GP: 0.82
9 podiums
0 wins
5 second places
4 third places
5 fourth places
5 fifth places
4 sixth places
1 pole position
1 fastest race lap

Qualifying score in 2001: Fisichella 13 / Button 4

Titles:
Italian Formula 3 champion in 1994.
Winner of the Formula 3 Monaco Grand Prix in 1994.

## F1 Record

Best classification in F1: 6th in 2000 (Benetton)
Best GP result: 2nd (Belgium 1997, Monaco and
Canada 1998, Canada 1999, Brazil 2000)
Best qualification in F1: 1st (Austria 1998)

1996: Minardi, 0 points, not classified
1997: Jordan, 20 points, 8th
1998: Benetton, 16 points, 9th
1999: Benetton, 13 points, 9th
2000: Benetton, 18 points, 6th
2001: Benetton, 8 points, 11th

F1 team-mates:
1996: P. Lamy
1997: R. Schumacher
1998, 1999 and 2000: A. Wurz
2001: J. Button

**First car driven?**
A Fiat 127 when I was 5.
**Road car?**
A Honda S2000 and a Honda Stream 7 seater.
**Favourite or dream car?**
I've got it yet.
**Best race car?**
All my F1 cars.
**Worst race car?**
The Formula 3 Ralt RT 36.
**Best racing memory?**
All my podiums are a wonderful memory. But I have particularly fond memories of my wins in the Italian F3 series and in Monaco in 1994.
**Worst racing memory?**
It has to be my retirement at the Nürburgring in 1999 when I was leading.
**Your racing ambition?**
To be world champion.
**Your favourite circuit?**
Imola.
**Your least favourite circuit?**
I don't have one.
**Your favourite driver of all time?**
Ayrton Senna.
**Your favourite driver of the current batch?**
I have a lot of respect for Michael Schumacher and Jacques Villeneuve.

**Favourite dish?**
Bucatini alla matriciana, a speciality pasta dish from Rome.
**Favourite drink?**
Coca-Cola and orange juice.
**Sports you participate in?**
Football, tennis, skiing, jogging, off-road cycling and the gym.
**Favourite sport?**
I'm interested in all sports, mainly football and the Roma team.
**Favourite sports star?**
I'm a fan of AC Roma, the football team and I know all the players well.
**What are your hobbies and interests outside sport?**
I love river fishing and playing billiards.
**Favourite films?**
Now I have a daughter, I don't really have time for the cinema.
**Favourite actor?**
I really like Roberto Benegni.
**What do you watch on TV?**
A bit of everything.
**Favourite music?**
As always, Elton John, Claudio Baglioni, Renato Zero and Madonna.
**Favourite reading matter?**
Car books and magazines.
**What is your favourite holiday destination?**
The Maldives.
**Favourite shopping city?**
It has to be the Italian cities of Rome and Milan.
**Do you have any pets?**
I have an aquarium and two birds.
**Outside of motorsport, do you admire anyone in particular?**
Cindy Crawford! (laughs)
**If you were on a desert island, what would you take with you?**
My wife Luna and my daughter Carlotta.
**Your ideal day?**
Going fishing and winning the football pools!
**What would you do if you were not a racing driver?**
I would have been a mechanic in a garage.
**What is the most important thing in life?**
Health and a happy family life.
**What do you like most about your job?**
I love being at the wheel.
**What are your main strengths?**
I'm a nice bloke.
**Have you got any faults?**
I'm not tough enough.
**Have you thought about your retirement from racing?**
To be a team manager and stay in racing.

# TAKUMA SATO

*Jordan Honda*

10

To date, Japanese drivers have not shone in Formula 1. The best result for one of them was Aguri Suzuki's third place in the 1990 Japanese Grand Prix.

Satoru Nakajima and, more recently, Ukyo Katayama have been the only two to make their mark, scoring points on several occasions.

This year, the land of the rising sun is counting on a young and very talented driver to put it on the map. Takuma Sato could well be on the threshold of a glittering Formula 1 career. Like Nakajima before him, he is backed by the power of Honda. This famous marque, with six world titles to its name, staged its F1 comeback in 2000.

Following the instructions of his engine supplier to the letter, the wily Eddie Jordan did not hesitate in saying goodbye to his old friend Jean Alesi to offer Sato the drive. This politically driven choice will no doubt prove useful at contract renewal time. Despite the fact he comes heavily backed, one should not ignore Takuma Sato's undoubted talent. Last year, he crushed all his rivals in the British F3 series. He made the most of the round which supported the British Grand Prix to show off his skills to the Formula 1 team managers. He went on to win the Zandvoort Masters, which ranks as a world final in the category. He did it again in Macau, showing he had nothing left to prove in Formula 3.

The young Japanese driver knows the road ahead is tough and littered with traps. But he is not lacking in determination and ambition. He is aware that, apart from his talent, his presence at Jordan will optimise relations between the team and its engine supplier Honda. He will be a valuable mouthpiece between the two organisations.

His first goal will be to match the performances of team-mate Giancarlo Fisichella. With a wry smile, he points out that Michael and Ralf Schumacher, Rubens Barrichello and Eddie Irvine all started their F1 careers with Jordan and that it cannot be a bad school… Takuma Sato wants to follow in their footsteps. A pretty good ambition.

## Takuma Sato

Date and place of birth: January 28, 1977 in Tokyo (Japan)
Nationality: Japanese
Lives: Marlow (Great Britain)
Marital status: Single
Height: 1,63 m     Weight: 60 kg

Internet: www.takumasato.com

### Career summary

Racing debut: 1996 (karts)
3rd driver for BAR F1 in 2001
GP debut: Australia 2002 (Jordan)

Titles:
Japanese kart championin 1997.
British Formula 3 champion in 2001.
Winner of the Marlboro Masters at Zandvoort and Macao Formula 3 events in 2001.

**First car driven?**
A Honda Civic when I was 18.
**Road car?**
An old Mini in England, and a little Honda Beat in Japan.
**Favourite or dream car?**
The Porsche GT3 and any Lotus.
**Best race car?**
The 2001 Dallara F3 with which I won the British championship, the Marlboro Masters at Zandvoort and Macau.
**Worst race car?**
I didn't like karts.
**Best racing memory?**
My 2001 Formula 3 season and my debut with Jordan.
**Worst racing memory?**
I want to forget them.
**Your racing ambition?**
To be F1 world champion.
**Your favourite circuit?**
Spa and Suzuka. I can't wait to try Monaco, because I love street circuits.
**Your least favourite circuit?**
I don't have any.
**Your favourite driver of all time?**
I used to watch Ayrton Senna on television in his McLaren-Honda days.
**Your favourite driver of the current batch?**
I don't want to have a role model. I want to be myself.

**Favourite dish?**
I like most types of food, including Japanese of course.
**Favourite drink?**
Fresh fruit juices and the occasional beer.
**Sports you participate in?**
Jogging, working out in the gym, cycling and skiing.
**Favourite sport?**
I love watching the cycling Tour de France.
**Favourite sports star?**
Kiroyasu Shimizu, a Japanese speed-skater.
**What are your hobbies and interests outside sport?**
Nothing special. I like going for walks and being with friends.
**Favourite films?**
I've got no particular preference when it comes to the cinema.
**Favourite actor?**
None really.
**What do you watch on TV?**
Sports programmes.
**Favourite music?**
Some Japanese bands and all sorts of pop music.
**Favourite reading matter?**
Japanese books and magazines.
**What is your favourite holiday destination?**
Hot countries, such as the south of Spain, Thailand, Malaysia and the south of Japan, which is really beautiful.
**Favourite shopping city?**
I don't have anywhere special in mind.
**Do you have any pets?**
A dog and a cat.
**Outside of motorsport, do you admire anyone in particular?**
My parents.
**If you were on a desert island, what would you take with you?**
My girlfriend.
**Your ideal day?**
To have no worries and to relax.
**What would you do if you were not a racing driver?**
I have no idea.
**What is the most important thing in life?**
To be compassionate and to be a trustworthy friend.
**What do you like most about your job?**
Driving.
**What are your main strengths?**
I never give up.
**Have you got any faults?**
My strength can sometimes be a weakness.
**Have you thought about your retirement from racing?**
Never…

# RACING HONDA

# BAR HONDA

On Tuesday, December 18, 2001, just a few kilometres from the Silverstone circuit where roadworks are in full swing, the British American Racing team presented its new car, the BAR-Honda 004. However, the new creation is not making the news. A terse press release is doing the rounds, informing the media that Craig Pollock, the man who created the team and friend and confidant of Jacques Villeneuve, has just been "let go". The two men had been inseparable and they heard the news just a couple of days earlier, while attending a ski race in Canada. The team was pretty much built around the former world champion, who that morning could only manage a very strained smile. The edifice had crumbled like a pack of cards. Pollock has been replaced by David Richards, like Jean Todt, a former rally co-driver. The immaculate Richards wears several hats. He looks after the TV rights for the world rally championship, runs the Subaru team with great success in this same discipline and now he has been appointed head of the BAR F1 team.

In 1998, he did not enjoy much success, when he took over the reins from Flavio Briatore at Benetton. Internal strife is nothing new at BAR. It is not the first time that conspiracy theories have been bandied about. Even if Formula 1 is essentially a business these days, sport must reassert itself. After the launch, Olivier Panis gave the new car a quick spin in the factory car park.

After the obligatory winter tests in Spain, the drivers seem reasonably happy. As is the case for so many teams, BAR is aiming for that fourth place in the championship: first place behind the untouchables. Important support from Honda and a comfortable budget should be enough to let this team improve. 2002 will be a crucial year. Without some decent results, this team's days are numbered. British American Tobacco will not keep pouring in millions of dollars for ever. It could be a case of cause and effect, just like Prost.

Address: British American Racing Honda
Brackley, Northants, NN13 7BD,
Great Britain
Tel: +44 (0)1280 84 40 00
Fax: +44(0)1280 84 40 01
Internet: www.britishamericanracing.com

Team principal: David Richards
Technical Director: Malcom Oastler
Number of staff: 350

GP debut: Australia 1999
Number of GP participations: 50
0 wins
0 pole positions
0 fastest race laps
Total points scored: 37
Points average per race: 0.74

Best classification in the Constructors' World Championship: 5th in 2000
Best classification in the Drivers' World Championship: J. Villeneuve, 7th in 2000 and 2001

Test drivers: Patrick Lemarié (France), Darren Manning (Great Britain), Anthony Davidson (Great Britain), Ryo Fukuda (Japan)

2001 classification: 6th (17 points)

## *The 2001 season summary...*

- 6th in the Constructors' World Championship
- Best result: 3rd (Villeneuve)
- Best qualification: 6th (Villeneuve and Panis)
- 17 points scored (Villeneuve 12, Panis 5)
- 23 Grands Prix finishes from 34 starts (Villeneuve 11, Panis 12)
- 6 points-scoring Grand Prix finishes (Villeneuve 4, Panis 2)

- Very strong budget.
- Energetic support from Honda.
- Very good, experienced drivers.
- Will to win.
- A team approaching maturity.

- Loss of Craig Pollock, the heart of the team.
- David Richards' lack of F1 experience.
- Has Jacques Villeneuve got bored?
- Team morale?
- The need to deliver.

David Malcom
Richards Oastler

# JACQUES VILLENEUVE 11

## *BAR Honda*

In the early Eighties, Craig Pollock was a sports teacher at the Beau Soleil school in Villars, in the Swiss Alps. One of the young boarders was called Jacques Villeneuve. After the death of his father, he had been sent there by his mother Joann, on the recommendation of family friend Patrick Tambay. A real friendship quickly developed between the young lad and the youthful teacher. It was now 1982. Twenty years later, the two men are still inseparable, linked by mutual respect. Craig Pollock became his manager and made a successful job of running his career. Together, they built the BAR team which was supposed to give Jacques a chance of taking a second world championship title. Then, for reasons which are still unclear, British American Tobacco decided last December it was time for Pollock to move on. It was a major blow to Jacques Villeneuve and in some ways, he has now become an orphan for a second time.

How will he react to this destabilising decision? The brilliant Canadian driver is fed up with just making up the numbers. The news of his friend's dismissal made for a lot of column inches and crazy rumours started to circulate. There was talk of Villeneuve switching to Renault or even Ferrari. Wisely, the man himself has decided to say little about the affair. Bearing in mind the early performance of this year's car and improvements due on the team's technical structure, he will make a decision shortly. In a world where uniformity is sadly the norm, the Canadian is a non-conformist. He cultivates the art of being different. Formula 1 needs this type of guy. He has all the attributes needed to make it work. He has a famous name, panache and he is scared of nothing. At the wheel of a competitive car, Jacques Villeneuve is desperate to win. He will not let the opportunity slip to make the point to those who have been quick in writing him off. Maybe the hour of vengeance is at hand.

# Jacques Villeneuve

Date and place of birth: April 9, 1971 in Saint-Jean sur Richelieu (Canada)
Nationality: Canadian
Lives: Monte-Carlo
Marital status: Single
Height: 1,71 m     Weight: 63 kg

Internet: www.jv-world.com

## Career summary

Racing debut: 1986 (racing school)
GP debut: Australia 1996 (Williams)

99 Grands Prix
209 points scored
Points average per GP: 2.11
23 podiums
11 wins
5 second places
7 third places
8 fourth places
6 fifth places
5 sixth places
13 pole positions
9 fastest race laps

Qualifying score in 2001: Villeneuve 11 / Panis 6

Titles:
CART champion in 1995.
Winner of the Indianapolis 500 Miles in 1995.
F1 World Champion in 1997 (Williams).

## F1 Record

Best classification in F1: World Champion in 1997 (Williams)
Best GP result: 1st (11 wins)
Best qualification in F1: 1st (13 pole positions)

1996: Williams, 78 points, 2nd
1997: Williams, 81 points, World Champion
1998: Williams, 21 points, 5th
1999: BAR, 0 points, not classified
2000: BAR, 17 points, 7th
2001: BAR, 12 points, 7th

F1 team-mates:
1996: D.Hill
1997 and 1998: H.-H. Frentzen
1999 and 2000: R. Zonta
2001: O. Panis

**First car driven?**
A Fiat Uno when I was 18. I hit a
policeman after going through a red light!
**Road car?**
A Honda S2000.
**Favourite or dream car?**
I rather like the Dodge Viper.
**Best race car?**
The 1997 Williams which took me to the
world title.
**Worst race car?**
The 1999 BAR.
**Best racing memory?**
My win in Indianapolis in 1995, and Jerez
in 1997 when I became F1 world
champion.
**Worst racing memory?**
It was in Phoenix in 1994, in Formula
Atlantic. I cut my car in half!
**Your racing ambition?**
It's very simple: to win.
**Your favourite circuit?**
Elkhart Lake in the United States.
**Your least favourite circuit?**
Detroit.
**Your favourite driver of all time?**
I have no heroes, but I have a deep
respect for Ayrton Senna.
**Your favourite driver of the current
batch?**
David Coulthard and Mika Salo are good
mates.
**Favourite dish?**
Pasta.
**Favourite drink?**
Milk and root beer.
**Sports you participate in?**
I am crazy about skiing. I also do quite a
bit of roller-blading and a lot of physical
training.

**Favourite sport?**
Skiing and ice hockey.
**Favourite sports star?**
The downhill skiers are incredible,
especially on the Kitzbühel run. As a rule, I
like people who do dangerous sports.
**What are your hobbies and interests
outside sport?**
Playing the guitar, writing and listening to
music and computer stuff.
**Favourite films?**
I saw Moulin Rouge recently, as well as
Lord of the Rings, Harry Potter, Mission
Impossible 2 and The Grinch.
**Favourite actor?**
Val Kilmer, Christian Slater and Meg Ryan.
**What do you watch on TV?**
The MTV music channel.
**Favourite music?**
At the moment, I'm into Lloyd Cole and
Train. The band Roch Voisine and the
music from the film Moulin Rouge.
**Favourite reading matter?**
I love reading, especially science fiction.
**What is your favourite holiday
destination?**
At home in Monaco or Villars, in the
Vaudoises Alps in Switzerland.
**Favourite shopping city?**
I hardly ever go shopping, except to buy
records and books.
**Do you have any pets?**
I have a cat called Eartha Kitten.
**Outside of motorsport, do you admire
anyone in particular?**
No one special.
**If you were on a desert island, what
would you take with you?**
I wouldn't want to be on my own.
**Your ideal day?**
Have a good breakfast and stay in the
sun, relaxing and then have a long lunch
which drifts into the afternoon with a
coffee.
**What would you do if you were not a
racing driver?**
Probably I would have done something to
do with music or my other passion, skiing.
**What is the most important thing in
life?**
Protection of my privacy.
**What do you like most about your
job?**
The danger, being on a knife edge, driving
on the limit.
**What are your main strengths?**
I like to be myself. I think I'm sincere and
spontaneous.
**Have you got any faults?**
I'm selfish and very untidy.
**Have you thought about your
retirement from racing?**
I'd play and compose music.

# OLIVIER PANIS

*BAR Honda*

**12**

After six years of devoted and loyal service to the blue of Ligier, which then became Prost Grand Prix, Olivier Panis needed a change at the end of 1999. He even found himself turning down an offer from Williams to take on the role of test driver with McLaren. This risk turned out to be a winning gamble. In the space of a few months, the Frenchman rebuilt his reputation. He acquired vast experience and metamorphosed into a contender. Ron Dennis, this top team's boss, waxed lyrical on the qualities of his test driver and did everything he could to hang onto him. But the siren call of a race seat was too strong.

BAR offered Olivier Panis a full-time drive alongside Jacques Villeneuve for 2001 and 2002. The man from Grenoble had won his bet. Since then, several other drivers have tried to go down this route, but with less success. In his new team, built entirely around the Canadian driver, Panis was never found lacking. At the start of last season, he was often quicker than his more illustrious team-mate and only bad luck robbed him of some podium opportunities. But then, after a few races, the BAR cars seemed to slide back down the order and they never featured again as front-runners.

Nevertheless, the future looks encouraging and Panis gets on well with Jacques Villeneuve. Panis is a well-integrated part of the team, which appreciates his qualities and his technical know-how. The BAR 004 has had a promising start in testing and it might just allow the only French driver on the grid to get the results he deserves. After a winter spent enjoying himself with his family, "Olive" is fired up and ready to go again.

## Olivier Panis

Date and place of birth: September 2, 1966 in Lyon (France)
Nationality: French
Lives: Varces (France)
Family: Married to Anne, 2 children (Aurélien and Caroline)
Height: 1,73 m    Weight: 76 kg

Internet: www.olivier-panis.com

### Career summary

Racing debut: 1980 (karts)
GP debut: Brazil 1994 (Ligier)

108 GP
61 points scored
Points average per GP: 0.56
4 podiums
1 win (Monaco 1996)
3 second places
1 third place
4 fourth places
5 fifth places
7 sixth places
0 pole positions
0 fastest race laps

Qualifying score in 2001: Panis 6 / Villeneuve 11

Titles:
French Formula Renault champion in 1989.
Intercontinental F3000 champion in 1993.

### F1 Record

Best classification in F1: 8th in 1995 (Ligier)
Best result in F1: 1st (Monaco 1996)
Best qualification in F1: 3rd (Argentina 1997 and France 1999)

1994: Ligier, 9 points, 11th
1995: Ligier, 16 points, 8th
1996: Ligier, 13 points, 9th
1997: Prost, 16 points, 9th
1998: Prost, 0 point, not classified
1999: Prost, 2 points, 15th
2001: BAR, 5 points, 14th

F1 team-mates:
1994: E. Bernard, J. Herbert and F. Lagorce
1995: M. Brundle and A. Suzuki
1996: P. Diniz
1997: S. Nakano
1998 and 1999: J. Trulli
2001: J. Villeneuve

**First car driven?**
A Honda Civic when I was 18.
**Road car?**
An old Mini in England, and a little Honda Beat in Japan.
**Favourite or dream car?**
The Porsche GT3 and any Lotus.
**Best race car?**
The 2001 Dallara F3 with which I won the British championship, the Marlboro Masters at Zandvoort and Macau.
**Worst race car?**
I didn't like karts.
**Best racing memory?**
My 2001 Formula 3 season and my debut with Jordan.
**Worst racing memory?**
I want to forget them.
**Your racing ambition?**
To be F1 world champion.
**Your favourite circuit?**
Spa and Suzuka. I can't wait to try Monaco, because I love street circuits.
**Your least favourite circuit?**
I don't have any.
**Your favourite driver of all time?**
I used to watch Ayrton Senna on television in his McLaren-Honda days.
**Your favourite driver of the current batch?**
I don't want to have a role model. I want to be myself.
**Favourite dish?**
I like most types of food, including Japanese of course.
**Favourite drink?**
Fresh fruit juices and the occasional beer.
**Sports you participate in?**
Jogging, working out in the gym, cycling and skiing.
**Favourite sport?**
I love watching the cycling Tour de France.
**Favourite sports star?**
Kiroyasu Shimizu, a Japanese speed-skater.
**What are your hobbies and interests outside sport?**
Nothing special. I like going for walks and being with friends.

**Favourite films?**
I've got no particular preference when it comes to the cinema.
**Favourite actor?**
None really.
**What do you watch on TV?**
Sports programmes.
**Favourite music?**
Some Japanese bands and all sorts of pop music.
**Favourite reading matter?**
Japanese books and magazines.
**What is your favourite holiday destination?**
Hot countries, such as the south of Spain, Thailand, Malaysia and the south of Japan, which is really beautiful.
**Favourite shopping city?**
I don't have anywhere special in mind.
**Do you have any pets?**
A dog and a cat.
**Outside of motorsport, do you admire anyone in particular?**
My parents.
**If you were on a desert island, what would you take with you?**
My girlfriend.
**Your ideal day?**
To have no worries and to relax.
**What would you do if you were not a racing driver?**
I have no idea.
**What is the most important thing in life?**
To be compassionate and to be a trustworthy friend.
**What do you like most about your job?**
Driving.
**What are your main strengths?**
I never give up.
**Have you got any faults?**
My strength can sometimes be a weakness.
**Have you thought about your retirement from racing?**
Never...

# RENAULT F1

Guyancourt used to be the kingdom of Prost Grand Prix, which went bankrupt one day after the launch of the Renault F1 team. Farewell Prost, welcome Renault was indeed a cruel twist of fate. On Sunday January 27, at the Renault Technocentre, just a few kilometres from the factory of the now defunct French team, the official return of the lozenge-badged company was celebrated with great pomp. Speaking to around 1,500 guests, Patrick Faure, President and CEO of Renault F1 is clear when it comes to the team's aims: "We have come back to F1 to win with a one hundred percent Renault team. We have decided to base Renault F1 in two sites, Viry and Enstone. I will be disappointed if the team does not finish in the top four in 2002. But more importantly, we have to close the gap to the top three teams, to win races on a regular basis in 2003 and challenge for the title the following year." The new Renault structure is unusual. The former Benetton base at Enstone looks after the chassis, something of an English speciality. Everything to do with the engine emanates from the Parisian suburb of Viry-Chatillon. Winner of the first ever Grand Prix, held in France in 1906, Renault has always adopted an innovative approach to Formula 1. In 1977, it was the first team to use a turbo engine and it also pioneered the V10 configuration in 1989, which went on to win six Constructors' World Championships from 1992 to 1997. The French constructor is keen on the motto, "passion, daring and innovation" and it sits well with the technical challenge it launched in 2001, running an engine with a revolutionary 111 degree V angle. Flavio Briatore and Jean-Jacques His can be relied upon to rally the troops and produce some good results this year. The driver line-up of Jarno Trulli and Jenson Button and test driver Fernando Alonso are champing at the bit to get started in their new colours. They have all the enthusiasm of youth, mixed with the requisite talent and experience to get the marque winning again in the short term, before trying to take the title with a car which is 100% Renault.

Address: Renault F1 UK
Whiteways Technical Centre, Endstone,
Oxon 0X74EE, Great Britain
Tel: +44(0)1608 67 80 00
Fax: +44(0)1608 67 80 00
        Renault F1 France
1-15, avenue du Pst. Kennedy
91177 Viry-Châtillon - France
Tel: +33 (0)1 69 12 58 00
Fax: +33 (0)1 69 12 58 17
Internet: www.renaultf1.com

Renault F1 chairman: Patrick Faure
Renault F1 UK MD: Flavio Briatore
Renault F1 France MD: Jean Jacques His
Technical Director: Mike Gascoyne
Number of staff Renault F1 UK: 390
Number of staff Renault F1 France: 250
Total number of staff: 640

GP debut: Great Britain 1977
Number of GP participations: 123
First win: France 1979 (J.-P. Jabouille)
Number of wins: 15
Number of pole positions: 31
Number of fastest race laps: 18
Total points scored: 312
Points average per race: 2.53

Best classification in the Constructors' World Championship: 2nd in 1983
Best classification in the Drivers' World Championship: A. Prost, 2nd in 1983

Test driver: Fernando Alonso (Spain)

- Renault's power and experience.
- An extensive budget.
- Excellent drivers.
- Highly-experienced technical staff.

- Revolutionary engine.
- A factory in England and another one in France.
- Identity and nationality of the team: French or English?
- Complex working structure.
- Is the engine now fully ready?

*Flavio Briatore*

*Mike Gascoyne*

# JARNO**TRULLI**

*Renault*

14

After two years good and loyal service at Jordan, Jarno Trulli has left his seat to fellow countryman, Giancarlo Fisichella. The two drivers, both protégés of Flavio Briatore, have quite simply swapped places. Thus, the Benetton team, sold to Renault, acquires another top Italian driver.

Racing is Jarno Trulli's life. Nothing else matters to him. Since he was eight years old, competition has been his everything. After brilliant results in karts, he won the German F3 championship, before moving straight into F1 with Minardi. He replaced the injured Olivier Panis in the Prost team, during the summer of 1997. He did not pass up the opportunity to lead the Austrian Grand Prix for a few laps and put himself in the spotlight. He continued his career with Prost for the next two years. But he was at the bottom of the wave and results were few and far between. However, always an opportunist, he made the most of the lottery which was the 1999 European Grand Prix to finish second in this unpredictable race. It is still his best result to date.

In 2000, he switched to the Jordan team which was in buoyant form. His team-mate, Heinz-Harald Frentzen had won two races the previous season. But that was a high-point which the team has never matched since, as the yellow cars were far from reliable. He did not get the results he was hoping for. However, he did excel in qualifying. At Monaco and again at Spa, he was quick enough to line up on the front row of the grid.

Last year, the scenario was repeated, with good grid positions going to waste, when reliability gremlins struck. There is no way his track record reflects his true ability.

He is planning to make up for lost time now he is with Renault. It is the first time he will benefit from the support of a major car manufacturer and his motivation is at a peak. He feels his time has come. Despite the effort he puts into his job, the man from Pescara never neglects the human side of life. He is a straightforward chap and there is no one more courteous or accessible in the paddock.

## Jarno Trulli

Date and place of birth: July 13, 1974 in Pescara (Italy)
Nationality: Italian
Lives: Monte-Carlo and Pescara
Marital status: Single
Height: 1,70 m     Weight: 60 kg

Internet: www.jarnotrulli.com

### Career summary

Racing debut: 1983 (karts)
GP debut: Australia 1997 (Minardi)

80 Grands Prix
29 points scored
Points average per GP: 0.36
1 podium
0 wins
1 second place (Europe 1999)
4 fourth places
3 fifth places
5 sixth places
0 pole positions
0 fastest race laps

Qualifying score in 2001: Trulli 15 / Frentzen-Zonta-Alesi 2

Titles:
Three-times Italian karting champion in 1988, 1989 and 1990.
World karting champion in 1991 (100 FK class).
Winner of the Ayrton Senna karting World Cup in 1994 and 1995 (100 FSA class).
European and North American karting champion (100 FSA class).
Karting World Champion in 1994 (125 FC kart class).
Italian 100 FA kart class champion.
German Formula 3 champion in 1996.

### F1 Record

Best classification in F1: 7th in 2001 (Jordan)
Best GP result: 2nd (Europe 1999)
Best qualification in F1: 2nd (Belgium 2000)

1997: Minardi and Prost, 3 points, 15th
1998: Prost: 1 point, 17th
1999: Prost: 7 points, 11th
2000: Jordan: 6 points, 10th
2001: Jordan: 12 points, 7th

F1 team-mates:
1999: U. Katayama (Minardi) and S. Nakano (Prost)
1998 and 1999: O. Panis
2000: H.-H. Frentzen
2001: H.-H. Frentzen and J. Alesi

**First car driven?**
A Renault Clio, when I was 18.
**Road car?**
I still have a Fiat 500 in Pescara and a Honda S2000.
**Favourite or dream car?**
I don't have one.
**Best race car?**
My Dallara F3 car in 1996.
**Worst race car?**
The 1998 Prost.
**Best racing memory?**
For the moment, it is still the Nurbürgring in 1999, when I finished second. It is my best F1 result.
**Worst racing memory?**
There are too many. I force myself to forget them.
**Your racing ambition?**
To get to the top.
**Your favourite circuit?**
Hockenheim is my lucky track.
**Your least favourite circuit?**
Monte Carlo, because it is too small for F1.
**Your favourite driver of all time?**
Niki Lauda and Alain Prost.
**Your favourite driver of the current batch?**
None in particular.
**Favourite dish?**
Pizza.
**Favourite drink?**
Coca Cola.
**Sports you participate in?**
Karting, cycling on the road, jogging, working out and sea canoeing.
**Favourite sport?**
Alpine skiing, the motorcycle grands prix and kart races.
**Favourite sports star?**
The cyclist Marco Pantani, who is a friend of mine, Di Luca, who comes from Pescara and in motorcycling, Biaggi, Melandri, Capirossi and Laconi.
**What are your hobbies and interests outside sport?**
I always take a laptop computer with me as it's a good form of escape.
**Favourite films?**
I liked the detective film "Seven" with Brad Pitt. There are others, but I can't remember the names.

**Favourite actor?**
I'm not a big cinema fan and it's just a distraction for me.
**What sport do you watch on TV?**
I watch the news a bit, to see what's happening in Italy.
**Favourite music?**
Pop, rock and blues, Elton John, U2, Sting, Zucchero, Vasco Rossi and Giovanotti.
**Favourite reading matter?**
I read newspapers a bit.
**What is your favourite holiday destination?**
To be honest, at the moment, I'm not thinking too much about holidays. I like relaxing at the seaside, which I can do at home in Pescara.
**Favourite shopping city?**
I don't really have a favourite. I like buying shoes and watches.
**Do you have any pets?**
In Pescara, I have four dogs and four cats.
**Outside of motorsport, do you admire anyone in particular?**
My family.
**If you were on a desert island, what would you take with you?**
A kart, a pair of overalls and a helmet.
**Your ideal day?**
When I am in Monte Carlo, I go cycling, motorcycling, canoeing and climbing. I also mess around with the computer, sending e-mails and I go to see friends.

**What would you do if you were not a racing driver?**
I've been karting since I was eight so…

**What is the most important thing in life?**
The family and being comfortable with oneself.
**What do you like most about your job?**
Driving and the fact a car is like a second family.
**What are your main strengths?**
I don't know.
**Have you got any faults?**
I am too much of a perfectionist.
**Have you thought about your retirement from racing?**
No, not yet.

# JENSON **BUTTON**

*Renault*

15

After karting and just two years of car racing, in Formula Ford and Formula 3, Jenson Button came straight to Formula 1, with Williams, in 2000. He put in some exceptional performances and threw into question all the preconceived notions about the accepted path to the top level of the sport. He may not have been the first driver to skip Formula 2 or F3000, as Piquet, Prost, Senna, Häkkinen and Schumacher all did the same thing without any problem, but he quickly got to grips with a grand prix car. It set off a scramble, as teams suddenly started looking for their next drivers in the lower formulae. Kimi Räikkönen and Felipe Massa are products of the Button effect. Buttonmania gripped England. As his contract with Williams could not be extended, he was "loaned" to Benetton last year. People did not rate poor Fisichella's chances against the young Englishman. But it was not to be. Powered by a technically innovative Renault engine, the Benettons had a disastrous start to the season. In this difficult climate and under pressure, Jenson was a shadow of his former self, dominated in every area by his team-mate. He seemed fragile and weak in adversity. His lack of experience was to blame. At the age of 21, he featured in all the newspapers and despite his best efforts, he lost concentration and was blinded by the trappings of his past success. He seemed to drop his guard and his performance suffered as a consequence. Flavio Briatore did not hold back from publicly expressing his disappointment in his driver's performance. In the space of a few weeks, it was hard to find anyone who had a good word to say about Jenson. But his 2002 contract was already in place and there was no perceived threat from the appointment of Briatore's new protégé, Fernando Alonso, to the role of test driver for Renault. Button knows he has already played his joker and has been given another chance - a rare occurrence in Formula 1. His driver's seat could soon become an ejector seat and he will have to shine when up against team-mate Jarno Trulli, who is no soft touch. But Button has regained his self-confidence and with a team committed to succeed, he knows he has to re-launch his career which looked so promising less than a year ago.

## Jenson Button

Date and place of birth: January 19, 1980 in Frome (Great Britain)
Nationality: Britain
Lives: Monte Carlo
Marital status: Single
Height: 1,81 m    Weight: 72 kg

Internet: www.jensonbutton.com

### Career summary

Racing debut: 1993 (karts)
GP debut: Australia 2000 (Williams)

34 Grands Prix
14 points scored
Points average per GP: 0.41
0 wins
1 fourth place
5 fifth places
1 sixth place
0 pole positions
0 fastest race laps

Qualifying score in 2001: Button 4 / Fisichella 13

Titles:
Six-times British karting champion, from 1993 to 1998.
British Formula Ford champion in 1998.

### F1 Record

Best classification in F1: 8th in 2000 (Williams)
Best GP result: 4th (Germany 2000)
Best qualification in F1: 3rd (Belgium 2000)

2000: Williams, 12 points, 8th
2001: Benetton, 2 points, 17th

F1 team-mates:
2000: R. Schumacher
2001: G. Fisichella

and mountain bike racing.
**Favourite sports star?**
I'm a fan of Liverpool footballer Michael Owen.
**What are your hobbies and interests outside sport?**
Surfing on the Internet, going shopping with my girlfriend and partying.
**Favourite films?**
Lord of the Rings
**Favourite actor?**
Julia Roberts.
**What do you watch on TV?**
I don't like television much, apart from sports programmes.
**Favourite music?**
Jamiroquai, Kool And The Gang, and most stuff from the 70s.

**First car driven?**
An Audi on a disused airfield, when I was 8.
**Road car?**
A Renault Laguna V6.
**Favourite or dream car?**
None at the moment.
**Best race car?**
The 1999 F3 car and its Renault engine.
**Worst race car?**
I'm only in my fourth year of car racing and I've never had a bad car.
**Best racing memory?**
In F1 in 2000, lining up third on the grid in Spa, and coming fifth at Silverstone.
**Worst racing memory?**
I finished second in the world super kart championship by a couple of seconds. In F1, 2001 was not an easy year.
**Your racing ambition?**
To be F1 world champion.
**Your favourite circuit?**
The Silverstone Grand Prix track.
**Your least favourite circuit?**
I don't like Imola.
**Your favourite driver of all time?**
Ayrton Senna and Alain Prost.
**Your favourite driver of the current batch?**
I have a lot of respect for Michael Schumacher.
**Favourite dish?**
Pasta.
**Favourite drink?**
Orange juice.
**Sports you participate in?**
Swimming, body boarding, all types of cycling and surfing.
**Favourite sport?**
Downhill skiing, major football matches

**Favourite reading matter?**
Motorsport magazines.
**What is your favourite holiday destination?**
Anywhere with a beach by the sea where it's hot.
**Favourite shopping city?**
Sloane Street in Chelsea, London.
**Do you have any pets?**
I'd like a dog, but I'm never at home.
**Outside of motorsport, do you admire anyone in particular?**
I like the singer Britney Spears.
**If you were on a desert island, what would you take with you?**
My girlfriend, a boat and some motorsport magazines.
**Your ideal day?**
Going shopping with my girlfriend and relaxing in Monaco.
**What would you do if you were not a racing driver?**
I would like to be a film director.
**What is the most important thing in life?**
Health and happiness.
**What do you like most about your job?**
The sense of speed, the competition and sharing my life with a team.
**What are your main strengths?**
I'm quite laid back and I don't judge others.
**Have you got any faults?**
I like racing too much.
**Have you thought about your retirement from racing?**
I would like to stay in racing. It's my passion.

# JAGUAR COSWORTH

In the summer of 2001, Bobby Rahal, who was trying to run his CART team in the United States, as well as heading up Jaguar's F1 programme, was given his marching orders. Ford called on triple-world champion Niki Lauda to replace him. The man with the famous red cap pulled down on his head is a legend in Formula 1 and he was given the task of bringing success to this equally legendary marque. The former Stewart team, renamed Jaguar at the start of 2000, can no longer afford to hang around getting its bearings. Lauda reckons his team will have to fight it out with Renault, BAR, Sauber and Jordan in 2002. The aim, as with so many teams, is to snatch that fourth place behind the inaccessible trio of Ferrari, McLaren and Williams. The Austrian champion insists that he can close the gap between his cars and the very best. With this in mind, he has called on Gunther Steiner, the man who oversaw the engineering and organisation for the Ford rally team, who has become the Technical Director, following Steve Nichols' eviction. To get a better understanding of what the cars are capable of and what his drivers are talking about, Niki Lauda even did a few laps at the wheel of a Jaguar on January 13, in Valencia. The test included a couple of spins. Up until this year, all Jaguar's wind tunnel research involved thousands of miles of travel to get to the Swif facility in California. It was a real nightmare for the aerodynamicists, but now it is over. The team has bought the old Reynard wind tunnel, not far from the factory. Tom Walkinshaw had hoped to sell them his, in order to amortise some of the costs of the Cosworth engines which will power his Arrows. Now he will have to find another buyer. There is no change on the driver front and they will be expected to get the most out of the cars. Last year, Eddie Irvine, one of the highest paid men on the grid, managed to make it to the podium with third place in Monaco, which pretty much saved the team's bacon. Pedro de La Rosa is keen to do well, having got a taste for points after coming fifth in Monza. Summing up the situation, Jaguar has to qualify in the first five rows in order to finish in the points on a regular basis. Ford, the Detroit-based giant, is persevering with its technical and financial support, without putting too much pressure on the team, despite the recession currently sweeping the United States. Ford has plenty of experience in motor racing and it knows better than most that success does not come quickly in F1.

Address: Jaguar Racing Ltd
Bradbourne Drive, Tilbrook,
Milton Keynes MK7 8BJ,
Great-Britain
Tel: +44(0)1908 27 97 00
Fax: +44(0)1908 27 97 11
Internet: www.jaguar-racing.com

Sporting Director: Niki Lauda
Number of staff: 345

GP debut: Australia 2000
Number of GP participations: 34
0 wins
0 pole positions
0 fastest race laps
Total points scored: 13
Points average per race: 0.38

Best classification in the Constructors' World Championship: 8th in 2001
Best classification in the Drivers' World Championship: Irvine, 12th in 2001

Test driver: André Lotterer (Germany), James Courtney (Australia)

2001 classification: 8th (9 points)

- Competence and experience in the shape of Niki Lauda.
- Excellent budget.
- Good drivers.
- New wind tunnel.
- Strong motivation.

### The 2001 season summary...

### Weak points

- 8th in the Constructors' World Championship
- Best result: 3rd (Irvine)
- Best qualification: 6th (Irvine)
- 9 points scored (Irvine 6, De la Rosa 3)
- 16 Grands Prix finished from 34 starts (Irvine 6, De la Rosa 7, Burti 3)
- 4 points-scoring Grand Prix finishes (Irvine 2, De la Rosa 2)
- 3 drivers entered (Irvine, De la Rosa, Burti)

- The need to deliver.
- A new organisational structure.
- Ford's financial worries in the United States.
- The sacking of Steve Nichols.

Niki
Lauda

# EDDIE**IRVINE**
*Jaguar*

At 36 years of age, Eddie Irvine is now the oldest man on the Formula 1 grid. When the Jaguar R3 was unveiled in Milton Keynes on 4th January, he announced he had never been fitter than after a winter spent training in Miami. There is an element of truth in his assertion that driving a modern Formula 1 car does not actually demand such a high level of fitness. He favours the theory that mental preparation and experience will allow him to dominate the young bloods currently pouring into the sport from all sides.

With 129 grands prix to his name, Irvine the rebel is the most experienced driver after the two Ferrari men. He is obviously a modest sort of bloke. "I have been in Formula 1 for over eight seasons. I won four grands prix with Ferrari and I was nearly world champion in 1999. I doubt that many of the other drivers have the same qualities and experience. I am quite intelligent, quite arrogant and a good enough driver to win. Only Michael Schumacher is better than me."

It is a succinct autobiography and a colourful one too. It is Irvine, the bad boy, the insolent one, who is endearing and fun. A self declared lady chaser, who dislikes the playboy tag, while enjoying the dolce vita, he seems to come from an age that has long since failed to be part of the sport. He takes everything life has to offer, but can also be brilliant behind the wheel, as could be seen by his drive to third place in Monaco last year, when he saved the team's bacon for the season. He did a great job of negotiating his contract with Jaguar and is one of the best paid men in F1.

"Irv the Swerve" is a loveable rogue and he knows this season is a critical one for his career. After two lean years, Jaguar has to get some good results. By his own admission, he knows that if he fails to deliver then he will be replaced like a faulty fuse. Irvine is a dinosaur; the last of a dying breed worth saving. Despite his age, he is as keen and fresh as ever. He is a wily opportunist who will always find a way to keep moving forward.

## Eddie Irvine

Date and place of birth: November 10, 1965 in Newtownards (Northern Ireland)
Nationality: Irish
Lives: Dublin (Ireland) and Milan (Italy)
Marital status: Single, one child (Zoe)
Height: 1,78 m    Weight: 70 kg

Internet: www.exclusively-irvine.com

### Career summary

Racing debut: 1983 (Formula Ford 1600)
GP debut: Japan 1993 (Jordan)

129 Grands Prix
183 points scored
Points average per GP: 1.41
25 podiums
4 wins
6 second places
15 third places
9 fourth places
7 fifth places
6 sixth places
0 pole positions
1 fastest race lap

Qualifying score in 2001: Irvine 11 / De la Rosa 6

Title:
Formula Ford 1600 champion in 1987.

### F1 Record

Best classification in F1: 2nd in 1999 (Ferrari)
Best GP result: 1st (4 wins)
Best qualification in F1: 2nd

1993: Jordan, 1 point, 20th
1994: Jordan, 6 points, 14th
1995: Jordan, 10 points, 12th
1996: Ferrari, 11 points, 10th
1997: Ferrari, 24 points, 7th
1998: Ferrari, 47 points, 4th
1999: Ferrari, 74 points, 2nd
2000: Jaguar, 4 points, 13rd
2001: Jaguar, 6 points, 12th

F1 team-mates:
1993, 1994 and 1995: R. Barrichello
1996, 1997, 1998 and 1999: M. Schumacher
2000: J. Herbert
2001: L. Burti and P. de la Rosa

**First car driven?**
I can't remember.
**Road car?**
An old Jaguar MkII and an XKR Coupe.
**Favourite or dream car?**
Ferrari GTO.
**Best race car?**
The most fun was the Le Mans Toyota in 1994. In F1, the Ferrari F399 in 1999.
**Worst race car?**
I want to forget them.
**Best racing memory?**
My first F1 win, in Melbourne in 1999.
**Worst racing memory?**
Monza 1999 and the 2000 season with Jaguar.
**Your racing ambition?**
To always be in a top team.
**Your favourite circuit?**
Suzuka.
**Your least favourite circuit?**
Silverstone.
**Your favourite driver of all time?**
Ayrton Senna.
**Your favourite driver of the current batch?**
I sometimes spend time with Jacques Villeneuve.
**Favourite dish?**
Sausages and peas, and Chinese food.
**Favourite drink?**
Miller beer.

**Sports you participate in?**
Jogging, golf, snowboarding, swimming and cycling.
**Favourite sport?**
Golf, sailing and cycling.
**Favourite sports star?**
Some golfers and cyclists, and motorbike racer Valentino Rossi, who is a great talent.
**What are your hobbies and interests outside sport?**
The Stock Market is a passion of mine. So far, it's always gone well for me. I also like fishing, flying my helicopter and playing the guitar. I also like pretty girls.
**Favourite films?**
I loved Snatch by Guy Ritchie, Madonna's husband.
**Favourite actor?**
Liam Neeson.
**What do you watch on TV?**
Films, documentaries and some sports programmes.
**Favourite music?**
All sorts of rock, and especially Van Morrison and U2.
**Favourite reading matter?**
I don't like reading.
**What is your favourite holiday destination?**
I love Miami. Life is very cool there.
**Favourite shopping city?**
Milan and New York.
**Do you have any pets?**
No.
**Outside of motorsport, do you admire anyone in particular?**
The American top model Christie Turlington. She's the most beautiful girl in the world.
**If you were on a desert island, what would you take with you?**
A very pretty girl.
**Your ideal day?**
A day on my boat, somewhere in the Mediterranean, with some good friends and sunshine.
**What would you do if you were not a racing driver?**
I would certainly be in business, playing the markets.
**What is the most important thing in life?**
To be happy and comfortable with yourself.
**What do you like most about your job?**
The ever present danger.
**What are your main strengths?**
I have too many to mention...
**Have you got any faults?**
None!
**Have you thought about your retirement from racing?**
I'd go fishing and travel and always be happy

# PEDRO DE LA ROSA

*Jaguar*

Pedro De La Rosa comes from a good family. Right from his first attempt at karting, his businessman father laid down the ground rules. "I won't stop you from racing, but don't look to me to help you financially." It makes his success all the more worthy.

So the young man from Barcelona had to make his own way in the world of motor sport. After time spent in the promotional formulae, he did not hesitate and moved to Japan to pursue his career. As did Ralf Schumacher, he won the Japanese F3000 championship, as well as the GT category. With nothing left to prove in the land of the rising sun, he returned to Europe. With backing from oil company Repsol, he became a test driver for Jordan and then made his Formula 1 debut in 1999 with Arrows. In this uncompetitive team, he managed to pick up three points in two years, while proving superior to his team-mates Takagi and Verstappen. Despite his worthy performance, he found himself out of a drive at the start of last year. Having accepted the role of test driver with Prost, he then quickly switched to the same job with Jaguar. It was a clairvoyant decision. Right from the Spanish Grand Prix, he made the most of a game of musical chairs to grab a race seat alongside Irvine, after Burti switched to Prost.

This difficult role did not prevent him from showing his true colours. In Monza, he was a strong ninth on the grid and fifth at the flag, his best result in F1. In 2002, Pedro De La Rosa has set himself the target of scoring points on a regular basis throughout the season.

He is an easy going, likeable chap, with a ready smile and acts like a true gentleman. In complete contrast to team-mate Irvine, he does not like to brag or express strong opinions in public. He admits that, sometimes, this quiet nature has gone against him, but he is not prepared to compromise his attitude to life.

## Pedro de la Rosa

Date and place of birth: February 24, 1971 in Barcelona (Spain)
Nationality: Spanish
Lives: Barcelona
Marital status: Maried to Maria
Height: 1,77 m      Weight: 75 kg

Internet: www.pedrodelarosa.com

### Career summary

Racing debut: 1988 (karts)
GP debut: Australia 1999 (Arrows)

45 Grands Prix
6 points scored
Points average per GP: 0.13
0 wins
1 fifth place
4 sixth places
0 pole positions
0 fastest laps

Qualifying score in 2001: De la Rosa-Burti 6 / Irvine 11

Titles:
Spanish Formula Fiat Uno champion in 1989.
European and British Formula Renault champion in 1992.
Japanese Formula 3 champion in 1995.
Japanese F3000 and GT champion in 1997.

### F1 Record

Best classification in F1: 15th in 2000 (Arrows)
Best GP result: 5th (Italy 2001)
Best qualification in F1: 9th (Italy 2001)

1998: Jordan (3rd driver)
1999: Arrows, 1 point, 17th
2000: Arrows: 2 points, 15th
2001: Jaguar: 3 points, 16th

F1 team-mates:
1999 and 2000: J. Verstappen
2001: E. Irvine

**First car driven?**
A Renault 5 when I was 9.
**Road car?**
A Jaguar XKR Coupe.
**Favourite or dream car?**
The Porsche 911 and the Porsche 917K which raced in the early 70s. I've got a replica of one. It's a fantastic car.
**Best race car?**
I hope it will be the 2002 Jaguar R3!
**Worst race car?**
The Lola in Formula Nippon in 1997.
**Best racing memory?**
My fifth place in Monza: my best F1 result to date.
**Worst racing memory?**
My British F3 season in 1994.
**Your racing ambition?**
To be F1 world champion.
**Your favourite circuit?**
Suzuka.
**Your least favourite circuit?**
Tsukuba, a kart track used for F3 in Japan.
**Your favourite driver of all time?**
Ayrton Senna.
**Your favourite driver of the current batch?**
I have a lot of respect for Michael Schumacher.
**Favourite dish?**
Pasta and paella. I hate English cooking.
**Favourite drink?**
Mineral water.

**Sports you participate in?**
Cycling, jogging, weight training, squash, karting and sailing.
**Favourite sport?**
Football, especially Barcelona FC. I go to their games from time to time.
**Favourite sports star?**
I am impressed by Michael Jordan's comeback in basketball. I admire soccer players Luis Enrique and Figo, who now plays for Real Madrid.
**What are your hobbies and interests outside sport?**
Reading and listening to music, when I'm not doing any sport.
**Favourite films?**
Bridget Jones and 15 Minutes, which I saw recently.
**Favourite actor?**
I love Anthony Hopkins, Uma Thurman and Meg Ryan.
**What sport do you watch on TV?**
Sport and good films.
**Favourite music?**
Some Spanish bands like Mecano and Bruce Springsteen, Kylie Minogue and modern music.
**Favourite reading matter?**
Adventure stories and biographies.
**What is your favourite holiday destination?**
I like going to Majorca with my family.
**Favourite shopping city?**
I don't like shopping! I let my wife do it. I do my shopping for the year in Montreal. I buy half a dozen pairs of jeans and some shirts.
**Do you have any pets?**
No.
**Outside of motorsport, do you admire anyone in particular?**
My wife Maria, my family and my friends.
**If you were on a desert island, what would you take with you?**
Maria...
**Your ideal day?**
To be happy with people I like.
**What would you do if you were not a racing driver?**
I would have worked in a small family business.
**What is the most important thing in life?**
To be happy and set oneself goals.
**What do you like most about your job?**
I like everything about it.
**What are your main strengths?**
I have strong opinions.
**Have you got any faults?**
I am too quick to think I understand people and I don't listen to them enough.
**Have you thought about your retirement from racing?**
I will go back to working in the family business.

# ORANGE**ARROWS**COSWORTH

# ARROWS COSWORTH

Last year, Tom Walkinshaw came close to pulling off a good deal. In signing Enrique Bernoldi, he secured his team's future thanks to support from energy drink, Red Bull. Walkinshaw, the energetic Arrows boss and former rugby player is tired of just making up the numbers and fighting for places at the back of the pack. He has therefore decided to get hold of the Ford-Cosworth engine, as used by Jaguar. He offered to sell them his wind tunnel at a favourable price to clinch the deal. Unfortunately, after protracted negotiations, the Big Cat opted in favour of the former Reynard facility.

To ensure his team's survival, he had to continue employing Bernoldi and his generous backer. This situation meant he lost a few sponsors and there were not many new ones on the horizon.

The technical side of the team is now directed by Sergio Rinland. Before leaving Sauber last year, he had designed an excellent car, which did the business for the Swiss team.

Unfortunately, the weeks dragged by and it was only on February 6 that Enrique Bernoldi gave the Arrows A23 its first run in Valencia. The following day, the team proudly announced that Heinz-Harald Frentzen had signed up and the German immediately completed his first laps at the wheel of the new challenger.

Thanks to the liquidation of Prost Grand Prix, Tom Walkinshaw has managed to recruit a driver whose experience will be beneficial. Last year, Bernoldi demonstrated good speed in qualifying. This season, both drivers are extremely motivated to help Arrows get out of the rut.

## Orange Arrows Cosworth

### Strong points

Address: Arrows F1 Team
Leafield Technical Centre,
Witney, Oxon OX8 5PF,
Great Britain
Tel: +44(0)1993 87 10 00
Fax: +44(0)1993 87 10 87
Internet: www.arrows.com

Team principal: Tom Walkinshaw
Technical Director: Sergio Rinland
Number of staff: 300

GP debut: Brazil 1978
Number of GP participations: 371
0 wins
1 pole positions
0 fastest race laps
Total points scored: 165
Points average per race: 0.44

Best classification in the Constructors' World Championship: 4th in 1988
Best classification in the Drivers' World Championship: D. Warwick, 7th in 1988

Test driver: none

2001 classification: 10th (1 point)

- Cosworth engine.
- An experienced driver: Frentzen.
- Walkinshaw's energy and drive.
- The arrival of Sergio Rinland.

### The 2001 season summary...

### Weak points

- 10th in the Constructors' World Championship
- Best result: 6th (Verstappen)
- Best qualification: 13th (Verstappen)
- 1 point scored (Verstappen)
- 18 Grands Prix finished from 34 starts (Verstappen 11, Bernoldi 7)
- 1 points-scoring Grand Prix finish (Verstappen)

- Budget problems.
- Car built very late.
- Hardly any winter testing.
- 2nd driver announced very late.
- Lacks support from a major manufacturer.

Tom
Walkinshaw

Sergio
Rinland

# HEINZ-HARALD FRENTZEN   18

*Arrows Cosworth*

Heinz-Harald Frentzen will remember 2001 for a long time. He made a good start to the year, scoring points on a regular basis. But not long into the European season, he lost his motivation. Frentzen and Eddie Jordan were seldomly on the same wave length, and the relationship between the two men soured. In the run-up to his home Grand Prix, to everyone's surprise he was fired. In the paddock, the news was the number one topic for conversation. But with Jean Alesi having slammed the door on Prost Grand Prix, Frentzen landed a new drive before Hungary. Despite his best efforts, he was never in a position to score points for the desperate French squad.

Whatever the extent of Alain Prost's financial trouble, he decided nonetheless to stick with the team. Tom Walkinshaw tried everything to hire the German, whose experience and talent would undoubtably lead to better days for Arrows. After the liquidation of Prost Grand Prix, things eventually went his way. On the day the announcement was made that he had been hired, Heinz-Harald Frentzen was already at work with his new team, testing at the Spanish track of Valencia.

At 34, he is fully aware that this season will play a crucial role for the rest of his career. The new boys are more and more agressive. False steps are off limits.

His considerable experience will prove invaluable to Arrows in the setting-up of the new A23. Three short weeks of testing will not be much to raise to the challenge.

For Heinz-Harald Frentzen, human relationships are paramount. When his self-confidence is on a high, he can deliver a stunning performance. Among his intentions is the desire to make Eddie Jordan regret his decision. The German driver has still not accepted his sacking which he considers illegal.

## Heinz-Harald Frentzen

Date and place of birth: May 18, 1967 in Mönchengladbach (Germany)
Nationality: German
Lives: Monte Carlo
Marital status: Married to Tanja, one child (Léa)
Height: 1,78 m    Weight: 63 kg

Internet: www.frentzen.de

### Career summary

Racing debut: 1980 (karts)
GP debut: Brazil 1994 (Sauber)

129 Grands Prix
159 points scored
Points average per GP: 1.23
17 podiums
3 wins
3 second places
11 third places
12 fourth places
9 fifth places
13 sixth places
2 pole positions
6 fastest race laps

Qualifying score in 2001: Frentzen 1 / Trulli 10, Frentzen 2 / Burti 0
Frentzen 3 / Enge 0.

Title:
German Formula Opel Lotus champion in 1988.

### F1 Record

Best classification in F1: 2nd in 1997 (Williams)
Best GP result: 1st (3 wins)
Best qualification in F1: 1st (2 pole positions)

1994: Sauber, 7 points, 13th
1995: Sauber, 15 points, 9th
1996: Sauber, 7 points, 12th
1997: Williams, 42 points, 2nd
1998: Williams, 17 points, 7th
1999: Jordan, 54 points, 3rd
2000: Jordan, 11 points, 9th
2001: Jordan and Prost, 6 points, 12th

F1 team-mates:
1994: K. Wendlinger, A. De Cesaris and J.J. Lehto
1995: K. Wendlinger and J.-C. Boullion
1996: J. Herbert
1997 and 1998: J. Villeneuve
1999: D. Hill
2000: J. Trulli
2001: J. Trulli (Jordan), L. Burti and T. Enge (Prost)

**First car driven?**
My father had an undertaking business. I drove one of his car when I was eight.
**Road car?**
A Mercedes SLK 230 and a BMW estate.
**Favourite or dream car?**
It would love it to be the Arrows…
**Best race car?**
The 1999 Jordan, when the team was at its peak.
**Worst race car?**
The Jordan EJ10.
**Best racing memory?**
My first Grand Prix win at Imola in 1997 and the birth of my son.
**Worst racing memory?**
My accident at Montreal in 1999, and the strange business at Jordan last year.
**Your racing ambition?**
To win Grand Prix races.
**Your favourite circuit?**
I don't know of a perfect circuit.
**Your least favourite circuit?**
Imola, despite the fact I won there in 1997.
**Your favourite driver of all time?**
Senna, Prost and Mansell.
**Your favourite driver of the current batch?**
No one in particular.
**Favourite dish?**
My mum's paella, fish and pasta.
**Favourite drink?**
Apple juice and mineral water.
**Sports you participate in?**
Jogging, training, mountain biking which I enjoy doing in Spain, water-skiing and jet skiing.

**Favourite sport?**
Football, mountain biking and leisure sports.
**Favourite sports star?**
Christopher Columbus , who produced an incredible feat when he discovered America.
**What are your hobbies and interests outside sport?**
I am passionate about all forms of aviation. I love radio-controlled planes, everything mechanical and engineering in general. I also like to film using a DVD camera.
**Favourite films?**
I haven't been to the cinema lately. I had other things on my mind…
**Favourite actor?**
I don't have any.
**What do you watch on TV?**
I don't watch it very often, except when it comes to sports.
**Favourite music?**
U2, the Stones, Abba, the Simple Minds, Phil Collins, Elvis Presley and rap music.
**Favourite reading matter?**
German (information?) newspapers.
**What is your favorite holiday destination?**
Places where I go to with the family.
**Favourite shopping city?**
I like buying duty-free on planes.
**Do you have any pets?**
I like animals, but I travel too much to have any.
**Outside of motorsport, do you admire anyone in particular?**
No one in particular.
**If you were on a desert island, what would you take with you?**
My wife Tanja and my daughter, a cook and some music.
**Your ideal day?**
To get up late, to be able to relax, play the sports I like and then have a nice meal…
**What would you be doing if you were not a racing driver?**
I would most certainly have worked with my father in his undertaking company.
**What is the most important thing in life?**
To be in good health and always optimistic.
**What do you like most about your job?**
I always dreamed of having an engine in my back.
**What are your main strengths?**
I tend to plan things ahead.
**Have you got any faults?**
I sometimes find it difficult to change my mind or my opinion.
**Have you thought about your retirement from racing?**
No.

# ENRIQUE**BERNOLDI** 19

*Arrows Cosworth*

Enrique Bernoldi made his grand prix debut with Arrows in 2001, after having first had talks with Prost. There is no doubt he is one of the most talented guys in the paddock. On track, he proved to be quicker in qualifying than team-mate Jos Verstappen. In the races, he will be remembered for the way he fought off the attentions of David Coulthard, during the Monaco Grand Prix, for more than half the race. Otherwise, his performance was nothing to write home about, but his car probably did not allow him to show his true colours. He was undoubtedly handicapped by his lack of experience, when compared with Verstappen, who is an old hand in this game. In the same car, Verstappen scored a point and made some really lightning starts. Relations between the two drivers was never a strong point. Bernoldi systematically refused to work together during the technical briefings. Both men accused one another of being at fault. With solid backing from the Red Bull energy drink, which has supported him since his Formula 3000 days, the young Brazilian's F1 future looks secure.

While Peter Sauber chose to go with Kimi Raikkonen, Bernoldi found a berth with Tom Walkinshaw, who welcomed him with open arms. In these difficult and uncertain times, a sack full of dollars still counts for a lot with many of the teams.

He therefore stays with Arrows, who this year will be running a more Cosworth engine, as supplied to the Jaguar team. Now he knows all the circuits on the F1 calendar, Bernoldi, who was brilliant in the lower formulae, must now confirm that early promise.

## Enrique Bernoldi

Date and place of birth: October 19, 1978 in Curitiba (Brazil)
Nationality : Brazilian
Lives: Salzburg (Austria) and Oxford (Great Britain)
Marital status: Single, a child
Height : 1,78m          Weight : 68kg

Internet :www.inriquebernoldi.com.br

### Career summary

Racing debut: 1990 (karts)
GP debut: Australia 2001 (Arrows)

17 Grands Prix
0 points

Qualifying score in 2001: Bernoldi 10 / Verstappen 7

Titles:
1990: Brazilian junior karting champion.
1996: Formula Renault Euro Cup champion.

### F1 Record

Best result in F1: 8th (Germany 2001)
Best qualification in F1: 15th (Brazil and Austria 2001)

F1 record:
2001: 0 points, not classified.

F1 team-mates:
2001: J. Verstappen

**First car driven?**
A Volkswagen Beetle when I was six.
**Road car?**
A BMW Z3 M.
**Favourite or dream car?**
The Ferrari Maranello.
**Best race car?**
This year's Arrows F1.
**Worst race car?**
None.
**Best racing memory?**
My win at Jarama in Formula Renault in 1996.
**Worst racing memory?**
Silverstone in F3000 in 1999, when I was on the back row.
**Your racing ambition?**
To be world champion.
**Your favourite circuit?**
Spa-Francorchamps.
**Your least favourite circuit?**
Budapest.
**Your favourite driver of all time?**
Ayrton Senna.
**Your favourite driver of the current batch?**
No one in particular.
**Favourite dish?**
Italian cuisine.
**Favourite drink?**
Sprite.
**Sports you participate in?**
I love water sports like surfing and jet skiing.
**Favourite sport?**
Football and tennis.
**Favourite sports star?**
The swimmer, Inge de Bruijn, the Brazilian soccer team, Gustavo Kuerten and Anna Kurnikova.
**What are your hobbies and interests outside sport?**
Brazilian beaches and jet skiing.
**Favourite films?**
I like American films.
**Favourite actor?**
Al Pacino, Laetitia Casta and the Brazilian actress, Isabeli Fontana.
**What do you watch on TV?**
Sports, MTV and films.
**Favourite music?**
All Saints and most music.
**Favourite reading matter?**
I don't like reading.
**What is your favourite holiday destination?**
Being on a Brazilian beach.

**Favourite shopping city?**
Milan.
**Do you have any pets?**
In Brazil, I have seven dogs, five pit bull terriers, a Bordeaux hound and a labrador.
**Outside of motorsport, do you admire anyone in particular?**
My father and my family.
**If you were on a desert island, what would you take with you?**
A Formula 1 car.
**Your ideal day?**
Doing some sport on the beach with friends and in the evening going dancing in a night club.
**What would you do if you were not a racing driver?**
I don't know.
**What is the most important thing in life?**
To be healthy.

**What do you like most about your job?**
Speed and the pleasure of driving.
**What are your main strengths?**
I think I am pretty consistent, straight and honest.
**Have you got any faults?**
I am sometimes too selfish.
**Have you thought about your retirement from racing?**
I would hope to be happy and spend more time with my family.

# MINARDIASIATECH

Last year, the little Minardi team was on the edge of the abyss, in a situation comparable to Prost Grand Prix. There was hardly a rush of saviours and the team was stagnating. Then, at the end of January 2001, Paul Stoddart appeared on the scene, the Australian having made millions in the aviation business. Already the owner of European Aviation, a team operating in F3000, he stepped in to save the little Italian squad, taking the reins at Minardi. With a 1998 specification Ford engine, rebadged as "European", the Minardis, in the hands of Alonso and Marques were not made to look silly. Then, like manna from heaven, Alex Yoong and his backers allowed the team to move forward. One lucky deal was followed by another piece of good fortune, when in Belgium, Asiatech, which was running the Peugeot engines, broke away from Arrows, to do a deal with Minardi. However, the departure of technical director, Gustav Brunner, bought for a huge bag of gold by Toyota, is an embarrassing blow. The new PS 02 car was designed by Loïc Bigeois, who used to work for Prost.

Alex Yoong's team-mate was announced right at the end of January. Prost's death throes delayed the nomination of Mark Webber, who could have come under threat from Verstappen or Frentzen. Paul Stoddart wanted an experienced driver and so his choice of fellow Australian Webber is hard to explain. But he is not a true neophyte, given that over the past few years, he has tested for Arrows and Benetton. The Minardi team's new livery will not be revealed until shortly before the Australian Grand Prix at a ceremony in the capital city of Yoong's homeland, Kuala Lumpur. The Minardi team is following Sauber's example of going for a young driver policy. Let's hope it is as successful.

### Strong points

Address: European Minardi F1
Via Spallanzani 21,
48018 Faenza, Italy
Tel: +39 0546 696 111
Fax: +39 0546 620 698
Internet: www.minardi.it

General Director: Paul Stoddart
Technical Director: Gabriele Tredozi
Number of staff: 160

GP debut: Brazil 1985
Number of GP participations: 271
0 wins
0 pole positions
0 fastest race laps
Total points scored: 28
Points average per race: 0.11

Best classification in the Constructors' World Championship: 7th in 1991
Best classification in the Drivers' World Championship: P. Martini, 7th in 1991

3rd driver: Andrea Piccini (Italy)

2001 classification: 11th (0 points)

- Asiatech engine.
- Growing budget.
- The will to improve.
- Drivers want to make a name for themselves.
- Dynamic team.

### The 2001 season summary...

### Weak points

- 11th in the Constructors' World Championship
- Best result: 9th (Marques)
- Best qualification: 17th (Alonso)
- 0 points scored
- 16 Grands Prix finished from 33 starts (Alonso 9, Marques 6, Yoong 1)
- 0 point-scoring Grand Prix finishes
- 3 drivers entered (Alonso, Marques, Yoong)

- Gustav Brunner has switched to Toyota.
- Drivers lack experience.
- No support from a major manufacturer.

*Paul* **Stoddart**

*Gabriele* **Tredozi**

# ALEX YOONG

*Minardi Asiatech*

At the 2000 Malaysian Grand Prix, a young local driver, Alex Yoong was wandering around the paddock. He had already left his fantastic homeland to tackle a couple of Formula 3000 races in Europe over the previous few years, as support events to the grands prix. He was in seventh heaven, rubbing shoulders with drivers he had only ever seen before on television. At the time, he certainly did not think that, just two years later, he would be one of them, racing with massive support from his home fans. Thanks to millions of dollars of Malaysian lottery money, he made his Formula 1 debut at the Italian Grand Prix at Monza, driving a Minardi. The manna from heaven, in the shape of dollars would buy him a drive for the whole of the 2002 season. He is, without a doubt, the archetypal pay driver. Yoong's father, the owner of the Shah Alam circuit in Malaysia, has put all his resources and those of his relatives to making his son's career a success. Even the family home was mortgaged to pay for racing. Without the backing of the Malaysian lottery and government money, who picked up the baton, all that investment would have come to nothing.

In Europe and Japan, from Formula Renault to Formula 3000, his results were never much to brag about. However, suddenly dropped into the harsh spotlight of the grand prix circus, he was not disgraced by his team-mate, Fernando Alonso, who is one of the big hopes for the future. He has done nothing special so far, but Yoong is honest enough to admit that he has to improve to be considered a real Formula 1 driver. He made the most of the long winter break to work on his physique which had room for improvement. This former water skiing champion is now living an amazing dream and the charming, ever smiling lad is facing a major challenge.

As the first Malaysian to drive in F1, he cannot afford to dash the hopes of all his countrymen. One can only hope he won't be crushed by the weight of that responsibility.

## Alexander Yoong

Date and place of birth: July 20, 1976 in Kuala Lumpur (Malaysia)
Nationality: Malaysian
Lives: Kuala Lumpur (Malaysia)
Marital status: Single
Height: 1,78 m     Weight: 68 kg

Internet: www.alexyoong.com

### Career summary

Racing debut: 1984 (karts)
GP debut: Italy (Minardi)

3 Grands Prix
0 points scored
0 pole positions
0 fastest race laps

Qualifying score in 2001: Yoong 0 / Alonso 3

### F1 Record

Best classification in F1: not classified
Best GP result: 16th (Japan 2001)
Best qualification in F1: 22th

2001: Minardi, 0 points, not classified

F1 team-mate:
2001: F. Alonso

**First car driven?**
A Proton Saga.
**Road car?**
I don't have my own car. I use my father's.
**Favourite or dream car?**
I have dreamed about cars.
**Best race car?**
The 2001 Minardi, my first F1 car.
**Worst race car?**
It has to be the Proton Saga. It certainly was not the best!
**Best racing memory?**
Racing in F3. There was always a good atmosphere.
**Worst racing memory?**
That would have to be my F3000 accident at Spa in 1999. I was taken away to hospital by ambulance and helicopter.
**Your racing ambition?**
To do my best.
**Your favourite circuit?**
Without hesitation, I would say Spa.
**Your least favourite circuit?**
Pembrey in Wales.
**Your favourite driver of all time?**
Ayrton Senna.
**Your favourite driver of the current batch?**
I don't have one.
**Favourite dish?**
Laska curry.
**Favourite drink?**
Sugar cane.
**Sports you participate in?**
Training and water skiing, which I used to compete in and golf.
**Favourite sport?**
I like all sports.
**Favourite sports star?**
I don't have one.
**What are your hobbies and interests outside sport?**
I like reading and playing the odd game of golf.
**Favourite films?**
I like the cinema and all sorts of films.
**Favourite actor?**
Morgan Freeman.
**What sport do you watch on TV?**
The film channels. I also like the National Geographic and Discovery Channels, which are very interesting.
**Favourite music?**
Pearl Jam.
**Favourite reading matter?**
Science fiction books.
**What is your favourite holiday destination?**
Going home to Malaysia.
**Favourite shopping city?**
Kuala Lumpur in Malaysia.

**Do you have any pets?**
My parents have dogs, which are sort of mine as well.
**Outside of motorsport, do you admire anyone in particular?**
I admire a lot of people, but I don't think it would be right for me to name them.
**If you were on a desert island, what would you take with you?**
My girlfriend.
**Your ideal day?**
Relaxing at home and being very laxy.
**What would you do if you were not a racing driver?**
I would have indulged my other passion and been a water skiing instructor.
**What is the most important thing in life?**
I can't answer that.
**What do you like most about your job?**
I have always loved motorsport. It's the most exciting thing I know. I like a competitive atmosphere.
**What are your main strengths?**
I am calm.
**Have you got any faults?**
I've got a lot. It would be easier to ask my family and friends to list them.
**Have you thought about your retirement from racing?**
I would just relax at home.

# MARK WEBBER

## Minardi Asiatech

Like Alex Yoong, his team-mate, Mark Webber attended the Australian Grand Prix in Adelaide as a kid. He was fascinated by Formula 1 and Alain Prost in particular. He stayed up all night watching the other races in the championship on television.

After dabbling in motocross, he decided to try his luck at karting. A chance meeting after a season of Formula Ford in Australia, saw him come over to have a go at racing in Europe, when he was 18. After finishing a strong third in the prestigious Formula Ford Festival in 1996, he won a free drive for the following season. It was not a great year, but it all came good in the end, when he won the Festival that year.

After driving in the Formula 3 race in Melbourne, he spoke to Mercedes motorsport boss Norbert Haug. A few months later, he was driving in the World Sports Car Championship at the wheel of an extremely powerful Mercedes. Teamed with Bernd Schneider, the company's favourite driver, he won five races. The following year almost ended in tragedy. During practice for the Le Mans 24 Hours, his Mercedes took flight down the famous Hunaudières straight at over 300 km/h, before landing on its roof. The next day, the same thing happened again. From that moment on, he vowed he would never step into a closed cockpit car again.

The year did have some good points however. He met fellow countryman Paul Stoddart, a self-made man who had just entered motorsport under the name of his business, European Aviation.

After two years in F3000, with some good results, he also took on the parallel role of test driver for Arrows and last year, he did the same job for Benetton.

At the end of January 2002, he became a full-time Formula 1 driver, after impressing in testing for Minardi. Big in size and in talent, he will see his dream come true, as his career kicks off at the Australian Grand Prix in Melbourne, in front of his home crowd. He will be the first Aussie to race in F1 since David Brabham in 1994.

His temperament has occasionally caught him out on the track, but he is a nice guy and richly deserves his place.

## Mark Webber

Date and place of birth: August 27, 1976 in Queanbeyan, New South Wales (Australia)
Nationality: Australian
Lives: UK
Marital status: Single
Height: 1,83 m     Weight: 76 kg

Internet: www.markwebber.com and www.webber-racing.co.uk

### Career summary

Racing debut: 1991 (karts)
GP debut: Australia 2002 (Minardi)

Titles:
Karting: NSW and ACT champion in 1992.
Formula Ford Festival champion in 1996.

**First car driven?**
A Toyota Corona in 1969.
**Road car?**
A Renault Scenic.
**Favourite or dream car?**
The BMW M5 and the Mercedes SLR.
**Best race car?**
My Formula 3 car.
**Worst race car?**
The F3000 car.
**Best racing memory?**
My win in the Monaco F3000 event in 2001.
**Worst racing memory?**
The Le Mans 24 Hour race in 1999.
**Your racing ambition?**
To win.
**Your favourite circuit?**
Spa.
**Your least favourite circuit?**
Barcelona.
**Your favourite driver of all time?**
Alain Prost.
**Your favourite driver of the current batch?**
Michael Schumacher.
**Favourite dish?**
Pasta.
**Favourite drink?**
Apple juice.
**Sports you participate in?**
All types of sports.
**Favourite sport?**
Tennis, squash, mountain biking, road cycling.
**Favourite sports star?**
Lance Armstrong.
**What are your hobbies and interests outside sport?**
I have none.
**Favourite films?**
I enjoy light-hearted films and comedies.
**Favourite actor?**
Jack Nicholson.

**What sport do you watch on TV?**
Documentaries and sport.
**Favourite music?**
Relaxing music and generally what's "in".
**Favourite reading matter?**
Autobiographies and biographies.
**What is your favourite holiday destination?**
I like going back to Australia.
**Favourite shopping city?**
Montreal and any of the big cities in Italy.
**Do you have any pets?**
No.
**Outside of motorsport, do you admire anyone in particular?**
Anyone who can overcome adversity.
**If you were on a desert island, what would you take with you?**
Loads of chocolate…
**Your ideal day?**
It would start with a nice leasurely breakfast, followed by some training in the morning. After a easy lunch, I would drive an F1 car in qualifying trim and go back home and flick the TV channels in the evening.
**What would you do if you were not a racing driver?**
I would have worked as a plumber.
**What is the most important thing in life?**
My family.
**What do you like most about your job?**
I love the speed and the adrenalin rushes.
**What are your main strengths?**
I am honest and down-to-earth.
**Have you got any faults?**
I can be very impatient.
**Have you thought about your retirement from racing?**
I will do loads of things for charity causes.

# PANASONICTOYOTARACING

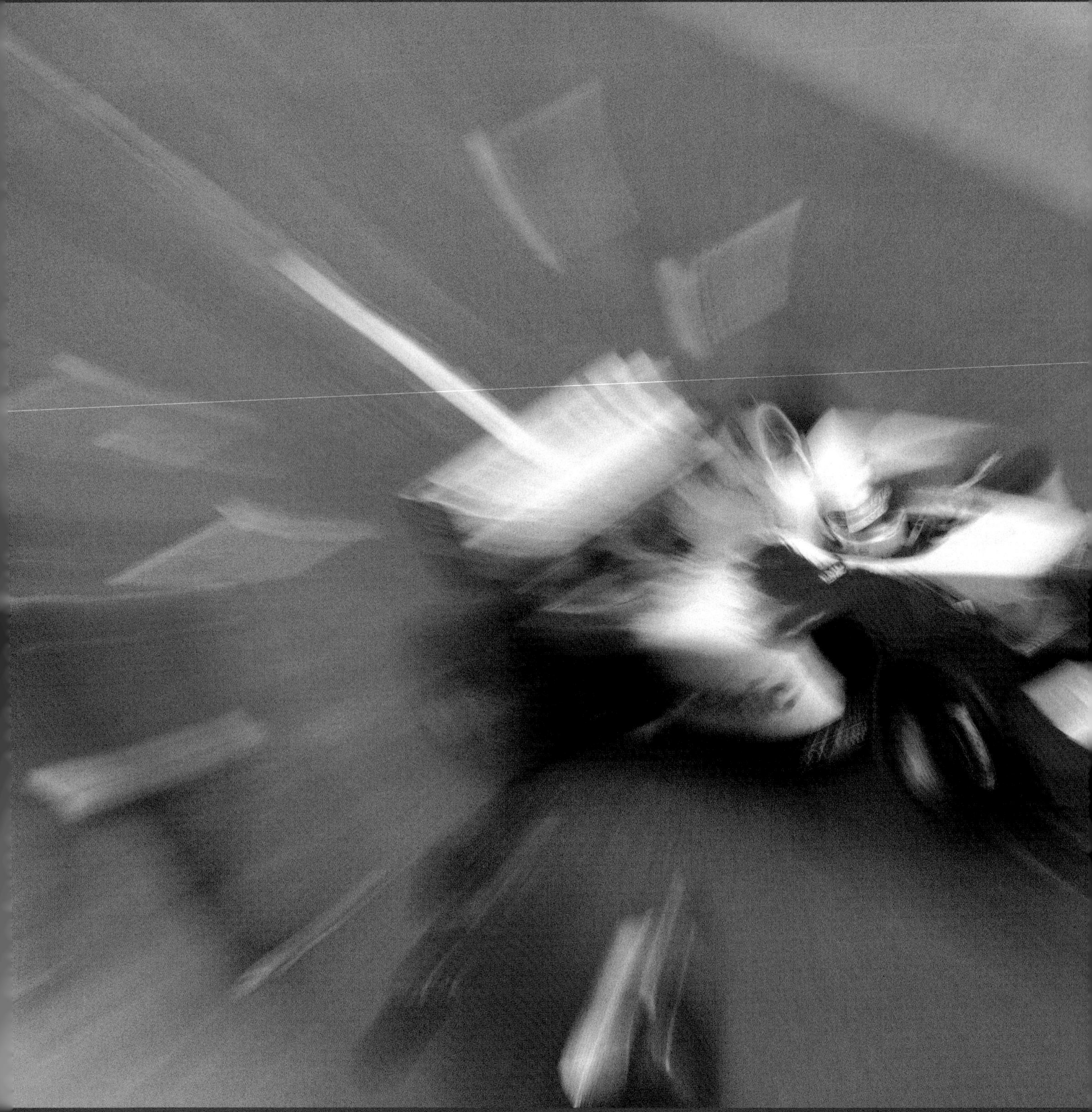

# TOYOTA

There were no half measures for Toyota's arrival on the Grand Prix scene. Like Ferrari, Jaguar and now Renault, the Japanese car company is taking the tough route into Formula 1, building both chassis and engine. The other giants of the car industry have not dared take on this challenge, preferring to supply engines to existing teams. They have left the job of producing the chassis to the specialist English teams.

Toyota were not prepared to go down this compromised route. Having announced, at the start of 1999, that it would be tackling F1 in the twenty-first century, it drew up every aspect of its plan on a blank sheet of paper. First off they built a new factory in Cologne, before beginning work on car and engine development. The race against time was the first obstacle for the "red and whites." The team is proud to describe itself as the "United Nations of F1", with over thirty nationalities represented in the squad.

After running for over a year with a test car, drivers Mika Salo and Allan McNish covered 21,000 kilometres on eleven Grand Prix circuits, as well as at its Paul Ricard base, in order to close the gap with its future rivals. Then, starting this year, Toyota began running at two circuits simultaneously to fine tune the new car. There are over a hundred staff working on the test team, which represents a colossal budget.

Despite its excellent funding, the new team knows that results will not come immediately. The Japanese characteristics of humility and wisdom will be useful.

Ove Andersson, the President of Toyota Motorsport, sums up the situation succinctly: "I think our aim for this year is to learn and to try and be respected by the rest of the F1 paddock."

Address: Toyota Motorsport GmbH
Toyota-Allee 7,
50858 Köln,
Germany
Tel : +49 (0)2234 1823 444
Fax : +49 (0)2234 1823 37
Internet : www.toyota-f1.com

General Director: Ove Andersson
Technical Director: Gustav Brunner
Number of staff: 550

GP debut: March 2002 (Australian GP)
Number of GP participations: 0

Test drivers: Ryan Briscoe (Australia), Franck Perera (France), Alex Storckinfeldt (Sweden)

- Considerable budget
- Excellent technical director.
- Great motivation.
- Experienced drivers.
- Very good organisation.

- Just starting in F1.
- Old drivers.
- Chassis and engine development work .

*Ove Andersson*

*Gustav Brunner*

# MIKA SALO

*Toyota*

In the 1990 British Formula 3 series, the Finns ruled supreme, with Mika Häkkinen taking the title ahead of fellow countryman, Mika Salo.

Häkkinen's career was about to take off. He joined Lotus in 1991 and then had a glorious time with McLaren. With no financial backing, Mika Salo was forced to head off for Japan. It was not until Suzuka in 1994 that he made his debut in F1 with the lacklustre Lotus team. He then spent four years with Tyrrell and Arrows, but they did not give him the chance to do well.

For a few weeks at the start of the 1999 season, he was unemployed. He learnt that his team had taken on the Japanese driver Takagi, along with his pot of gold. But injuries to Ricardo Zonta and then Michael Schumacher allowed him to relaunch his career. He did a great job as stand-in at Ferrari. In the German Grand Prix, he was in the lead until he let team-mate Eddie Irvine by, as the Irishman was in the running for the title. He suddenly found himself on the podium on a regular basis. His work was appreciated by the Scuderia, which helped get him a drive with Sauber for 2000. Unfortunately, success did not follow.

Mika Salo gradually slipped down the order, worn out by years of fighting at the back of the grid. The birth of Toyota's F1 team has given him the chance to start off on another exciting challenge.

At 35, he is tackling the job with great enthusiasm and is determined to provide the Japanese constructor with some good results, before hanging up his helmet.

## Mika Salo

Date and place of birth: November 30, 1966 in Helsinki (Finland)
Nationality: Finnish
Lives: London (Great Britain)
Marital status: Married to Noriko, one child (Max)
Height: 1,75 m     Weight: 69 kg

Internet: www.mikasalo.net

### Career summary

Racing debut: 1978 (karts)
GP debut: Japan 1994 (Lotus)

93 Grands Prix
31 points scored
Points average per GP: 0.33
2 podiums
0 wins
1 second place
1 third place
1 fourth places
7 fifth places
4 sixth places
0 pole positions
0 fastest race laps

Titles:
European Formule Ford, Scandinavian Formula Ford and Finnish Formula Ford champion in 1988.

### F1 Record

Best classification in F1: 10th in 1999 (BAR and Ferrari)
Best GP result: 2nd (Germany 1999)
Best qualification in F1: 4th (Germany 1999)

1994: Lotus, 0 points, not classified
1995: Tyrrell, 5 points, 14th
1996: Tyrrell, 5 points, 13th
1997: Tyrrell, 2 points, 16th
1998: Arrows, 3 points, 13th
1999: BAR and Ferrari, 10 points, 10th
2000: Sauber, 6 points, 11th
2001: Toyota, test driver, did not race

F1 team-mates:
1994: A. Zanardi
1995: U. Katayama and G. Tarquini
1996: U. Katayama
1997: J. Verstappen
1998: P. Diniz
1999: J. Villeneuve and E. Irvine
2000: P. Diniz

**First car driven?**
I drove a Datsun 100 when I was six, sitting on my father's knee. Later, I went off on my own in an Austin Mini.
**Road car?**
For contractual reasons, I drive Toyotas. I have a Lexus, and also a Ferrari Maranello.
**Favourite or dream car?**
None really.
**Best race car?**
The 1999 Ferrari F 399.
**Worst race car?**
Sadly, I've had too many to mention.
**Best racing memory?**
The Formula Ford days. I was relaxed and carefree.
**Worst racing memory?**
Definitely Spa in 1998 with Arrows. I broke two cars in practice and could not race.
**Your racing ambition?**
To indulge my love of driving.
**Your favourite circuit?**
Suzuka.
**Your least favourite circuit?**
Also in Japan, Mount Fuji.
**Your favourite driver of all time?**
James Hunt.
**Your favourite driver of the current batch?**
Jacques Villeneuve and David Coulthard are good mates.
**Favourite dish?**
Pasta.
**Favourite drink?**
Milk.
**Sports you participate in?**
Training, cycling, snowboarding and skidoos in Finland.
**Favourite sport?**
Ice hockey and snowboard competitions.
**Favourite sports star?**
I am a fan of some ice hockey teams, and player Teemu Selanne.
**What are your hobbies and interests outside sport?**
I love music. I have thousands of CDs and I like playing the guitar.

**Favourite films?**
There are too many to name. I like James Bond and action films. The last one I remember was Pearl Harbour.
**Favourite actor?**
Robert de Niro and Jennifer Lopez.

**What do you watch on TV?**
I tend to zap between channels a lot.
**Favourite music?**
Hard rock like Led Zeppelin and AC/DC.
**Favourite reading matter?**
Comic books.
**What is your favourite holiday destination?**
No question, that would be Brazil.
**Favourite shopping city?**
I don't like shopping. My wife Noriko does it for me.
**Do you have any pets?**
Yes, a dog.
**Outside of motorsport, do you admire anyone in particular?**
A lot of people, especially any sports people who push themselves to the limit to succeed.
**If you were on a desert island, what would you take with you?**
My wife, my son and lots to eat.
**Your ideal day?**
Doing nothing. I like playing with my son Max and my dog.
**What would you do if you were not a racing driver?**
I have never asked myself that question.
**What is the most important thing in life?**
Health.
**What do you like most about your job?**
The sense of freedom.
**What are your main strengths?**
That's for you to say!
**Have you got any faults?**
Lots of nasty things…
**Have you thought about your retirement from racing?**
Not yet.

# ALLAN McNISH

*Toyota*

23

Allan McNish's story is worth telling, which is rare in Formula 1 these days. In 1990, after Formula 3, he became McLaren's test driver, working with Ayrton Senna. At the same time, he competed in F3000, in preparation for his time at the top. His future was all mapped out, but a lack of backing saw it collapse around him.

He was forced to spend another season in F3000, where a totally uncompetitive car ruined his chances and the rest of his career. Later he became a test driver for Benetton, but there was no hope of promotion to full-time driver. He worked out that single seaters were not for him and turned to endurance racing. He won Le Mans and Daytona, and built up a good track record in this discipline, with Toyota, Porsche and Audi.

It came as a real surprise when the Japanese car manufacturer, recognising his ability, appointed him as development driver for its F1 project, alongside Mika Salo. The dream then became reality when he was nominated as a race driver for Toyota's F1 debut. At 32 years of age, the little Scotsman would finally make it onto the grid, twelve years after testing for McLaren.

What a great reward! In a world where money talks, the arrival of Allan McNish is a real breath of fresh air. For once, human qualities have dominated the dollar. This courteous, ever smiling little man can be counted on to show he is worthy of the chance he has been given.

He has never been embarrassed by Mika Salo during Toyota's test programme. And, no doubt, he will remember that a certain Damon Hill made his Formula 1 debut at the same age and we all know how that story ended.

## Allan McNish

Date and place of birth: December 29, 1969 in Dumfries (Scotland)
Nationality: British
Lives: London (Great Britain)
Marital status: Engaged to Kinny
Height: 1,65 m     Weight: 58 kg

Internet: www.allanmcnish.com

### Career summary

Racing debut: 1981 (karts)
GP debut: Australia 2002 (Toyota)

Titles:
British Formula Vauxhall Lotus champion in 1988.
Winner of Le Mans 24 Hours in 1997 (Porsche).
Winner of the American Le Mans Series in 2000 (Audi).

### F1 Record

McLaren test driver in 1990 and 1991
Benetton test driver in 1993, 1994 and 1996
Toyota development driver in 2000
Toyota test driver in 2001

*First car driven?*
If my memory serves me well, it was an Alfa Romeo Alfasud.
*Road car?*
A Toyota Lexus.
*Favourite or dream car?*
The new Porsche. I was involved in its development.
*Best race car?*
This year's F1 Toyota.
*Worst race car?*
The F3000 Lola in 1991.
*Best racing memory?*
The Le Mans podium in 1997 with Aiello and Johansson.
*Worst racing memory?*
My accident at Donington in 1990.
*Your racing ambition?*
To win.
*Your favourite circuit?*
Spa and Suzuka.
*Your least favourite circuit?*
Albacete in Spain.
*Your favourite driver of all time?*
Clark and Stewart when I was a kid, then Prost and Senna and finally, Michele Alboreto, whom I knew at Audi. He was a real gentleman.
*Your favourite driver of the current batch?*
Michael Schumacher for his results and Nick Heidfeld, who sent me a good luck card.
*Favourite dish?*
I like all types of food.
*Favourite drink?*
I'm Scottish, so I like whisky! But usually, I drink water and tea.
*Sports you participate in?*
Training and water skiing which I am really keen on.

*Favourite sport?*
I like football, especially Glasgow Celtic and Nottingham Forest.
*Favourite sports star?*
Giacomo Agostini.
*What are your hobbies and interests outside sport?*
I just like to relax.
*Favourite films?*
I like action films which don't involve too much thought. I watch a film to have a good time.
*Favourite actor?*
Clint Eastwood and Cameron Diaz.
*What do you watch on TV?*
News and comedies.
*Favourite music?*
Lenny Kravitz and most rock music.
*Favourite reading matter?*
Autobiographies and novels.
*What is your favourite holiday destination?*
I like hot places. This winter I went to Barbados. It was fantastic. There was no telephone or mail.
*Favourite shopping city?*
San Francisco.
*Do you have any pets?*
A cat.
*Outside of motorsport, do you admire anyone in particular?*
Cyclist Lance Armstrong.
*If you were on a desert island, what would you take with you?*
A radio to keep in touch with the outside world.
*Your ideal day?*
To get up without an alarm clock, to relax in the morning and then spend the rest of the day and evening with friends.
*What would you do if you were not a racing driver?*
Part of my family sells cars and the others sell farming equipment, so I would have gone into that business.
*What is the most important thing in life?*
Being happy.
*What do you like most about your job?*
Being able to express myself, and meeting people.
*What are your main strengths?*
Determination.
*Have you got any faults?*
Too much determination can sometimes be a fault.
*Have you thought about your retirement from racing?*
I live from day to day. I never make long-term plans. I make the most of the moment.

MAGAZINES

"la Caixa"

3:19:51

VOLTA

1
2
3
4
5
6
7
8
9
10

# CHANGES4
## 2002

## On the technical front

2002 will be a year of stability on the regulation front. In fact, teams could even start the season with last year's cars. Ferrari has certainly considered this option. Perfecting new technologies can be painful. It could be a better plan to race with a well-proven package until the new car is totally reliable. However, there are a few changes to the rule book.

### 2002 Sporting regulations:
- Telemetry can now be bi-directional between car and pit. This means that some settings on the car can be changed from the pit wall.

### 2002 Technical regulations:
- Start light detection systems are banned.
- Electronically-controlled power steering is banned.

### 2002 Safety regulations
- The start procedure system must be posted on the car's dashboard.
- A warning system will be put in place to inform drivers and teams of a speed limit imposed on part of the circuit, following an incident or accident.
- The size of the rear view mirrors is increased by 20%, from 120x50 cm to 150x50 cm.
- The rear deformable structure has to pass a side-impact test.
- The wheel retaining cables have to be 20% stronger.
- The size of the rear light is increased by 50%.

## On the sporting front

The teams are pretty evenly divided into Bridgestone and Michelin runners. It will be a close-fought contest between them, and one can expect improvements on the tyre front to produce even quicker lap times. Research is costly as teams strive to find a tenth of a second advantage over the opposition. Tyres can sometimes make a difference measured in second. Some circuits will throw up some real surprises, but no one will complain. The major event this year on the tyre front, is McLaren's switch from Bridgestone to Michelin.

Bridgestone will supply five teams :

| | | |
|---|---|---|
| Ferrari | Jordan | BAR |
| Arrows | Sauber | |

Michelin will supply six teams:

| | | |
|---|---|---|
| McLaren | Williams | Benetton |
| Jaguar | Minardi | Toyota |

*Felipe Massa*

- Tarso Marques.
- Gaston Mazzacane.
- Tomas Enge, from Prost to F3000.
- Ricardo Zonta.

### Back in Formula One:
- Mika Salo from test driver to Toyota race driver.

### Rookies:
- Allan McNish, from Audi to Toyota.
- Felipe Massa, from Euro 3000 to Sauber.
- Takuma Sato, from F3 to Jordan.
- Mark Webber, from F3000 to Minardi.

*Takuma Sato*

*Fernando Alonso*

## *Team personnel*

### Main transfers:
- Geoff Willis, from Williams to BAR.
- Gabriele Delli Colli, from Jordan to Ferrari.
- Chris Cooney, from Jordan to Renault.
- Peter Heard, from Jordan to Renault.
- Gianni Sale, from Prost to Jordan.
- Giorgio Ascanelli, from Ferrari to Maserati.
- Claudio Berro, from Ferrari to Maserati.
- Guenther Steiner, from Ford Rally to Jaguar.
- Humphrey Corbett, from Jaguar to Toyota.
- Sergio Rinland, from Sauber to Arrows.
- John Walton, from Prost to Minardi.
- Gary Anderson, from Reynard USA to Jordan.
- Gustav Brunner, from Minardi to Toyota.

*With the Prost Grand Prix team going bankrupt, there are bound to be several other changes in the early part of the season.

### No longer in Formula One:
- Jo Ramirez, from McLaren to retirement.
- Bobby Rahal, from Jaguar.
- Steve Nichols, from Jaguar.
- Craig Pollock, from BAR.
- Jim Vale, from Jordan.
- Alain Prost, from Prost.

### New boys:
- The Toyota team.

*Allan McNish*

# *On the human front*

## *The drivers*

### The transfers:
- Jarno Trulli, from Jordan to Renault.
- Giancarlo Fisichella, from Benetton to Jordan.
- Kimi Räikkönen, from Sauber to McLaren.
- Luciano Burti, from Prost to Ferrari (test driver).
- Fernando Alonso, from Minardi to Renault (3rd driver).

### No longer in Formula One:
- Mika Häkkinen, enjoying a sabbatical in 2002.
- Jean Alesi, from Jordan to Mercedes in the DTM.

# F1 NUMBERS

## On a more general note:

- Toyota arrives.
- Renault officially returns.
- The Prost team disappears after being declared bankrupt.
- The old Ford engine, dating back to 1998, disappears from the Grand Prix scene.
- The Arrows team switches from Asiatech to Cosworth engines.
- Major sponsors (Vodafone at Ferrari, 7 UP at Williams) arrive in Formula One. ■

THE PARTS PRICE LIST (All prices in Euros)

| | |
|---|---|
| Brake pad (each) | 160 |
| Brake disc (each) | 1450 |
| Steering wheel | 80,000 |
| Seat | 3,000 |
| Safety harness | 2,800 |
| Rear view mirror (each) | 610 |
| Tyre (each) | 2,500 |
| Rim | 700 |
| Wheel nut | 470 |
| Suspension wishbone (each) | 3,000 |
| Front suspension | 15,000 |
| Damper | 1,700 |
| Pedal box | 2,000 |
| Pedals (full set) | 1,800 |
| Steering system | 13,400 |
| Hub carrier | 10,700 |
| Hub | 10,000 |
| Nose | 14,000 |
| Front wing | 5,000 |
| Rear wing | 25,000 |
| Fuel cell | 17,000 |
| Extinguishers | 7,600 |
| Radiator (each) | 4,700 |
| Engine cover | 10,700 |
| Complete bodywork | 33,000 |

*Already used by CART drivers, the "Hans" system protects cervical vertebrae in case of accident.*

| | |
|---|---|
| Floor | 2,000 |
| Exhausts | 10,000 |
| Rear suspension | 15,250 |
| Carbon monocoque | 100,000 |
| Telemetry system | 130,000 |
| Gearbox | 125,000 |
| Gear (each) | 2,500 |
| Clutch | 9,100 |
| Electronic control box | 7,000 |
| Wiring loom | 9,200 |
| ECU | 4,600 |
| Telemetry transmitter | 1,000 |
| Cables | 750 |
| Engine (factory-supplied) | 350,000 |

*The cost of a factory-supplied engine can only be an approximation. Research and development budgets are not included in this assessment. These days, it is impossible to obtain accurate information about engines. All that can be said is that engines weigh less than 100 kilos. It is estimated that the best of the current generation have a power output close to 900 bhp.

On average, over the course of a year, a team running two cars will use one thousand tyres. During a Grand Prix weekend, each driver can use 40 dry weather tyres and 28 rain tyres.

Some teams do not have to pay for their tyres, as they represent one of the manufacturers. Those who do have to pay for their tyres spend over two million Euros a year. It is rumoured that the Bridgestone tyres are less expensive than Michelins.

A driver's fireproof overalls cost around 3,000 Euros, depending on design and artwork.
A driver uses between 6 and 36 overalls a year, depending on sponsor requirements (teams backed by a tobacco company must respect anti-tobacco laws in some countries).
On top of that, the team will order a further 45 overalls for the mechanics to wear during pit-stops.
A pair of racing boots costs around 100 Euros and a driver will get through 10 pairs in a season.
Gloves cost around 50 Euros and drivers use about twenty pairs a year. A set of underwear comes in at 80 Euros and a driver will need twenty sets.
All clothing suppliers market these products in an aggressive way. In the past, drivers bought their own clothing, but the marketing value of F1 means that all teams now negotiate free supply deals, and manufacturers are happy to oblige and are even prepared to paying additional sponsorship money. A presence in Formula 1 in association with a top Grand Prix team usually pays off in advertising terms.

Some drivers have personal clothing sponsorship deals, especially with the crash helmet manufacturers. Four manufacturers of head protection are currently involved in the sport: Bell from the United States, Bieffe from Italy, Japan's Arai and, a newcomer on the scene last year, Schuberth from Germany. The four suppliers seem to coexist happily and the first three on the list have the lion's share of the grid. The German company made a discrete appearance, working mainly for BMW and its products are not readily available for sale. Nick Heidfeld was the first to try them and was followed by Ralf and then Michael Schumacher, who decided to go for a home-grown product.
The cost of an F1 helmet varies according to the make. The less pricy is the Bieffe (800 Euros), followed by Arai (1,100 Euros) and finally Bell (2,300 Euros). The Schuberth helmets are not for sale. Representatives of these companies attend the races to service their products. Each driver has a certain allocation per year. The more famous the driver, the greater the number of helmets handed out per year. Last year, Michael Schumacher and Jacques Villeneuve got a new one at each of the 17 Grands Prix. The rear of the helmet usually bears the national flag and the year, so that it can be easily identified.
Finally, a visor cost approximately 130 Euros. ∎

# DANGER AHEAD

In an unrelenting way, the gap is getting bigger between the "haves" and the "have-nots". The rules that apply to the world in general hold true in Formula One. The disappearance of the Prost team is the latest example of this phenomenon. Inflation is galloping and the arms race is without limits. The cost of designing and building a Grand Prix car is now reaching astronomical levels. Nothing is too expensive if it shows how important a team is. Motor-homes are now mobile hotels and the costs continue to spiral upwards. After the long post-season break in November and December 2001, the teams have worked like mad to make up for lost time. Test sessions went on week after week in Barcelona and Valencia. The heavy artillery was out in force. As an example, for the test during the last week of January at the Circuit de Catalunya, Scuderia Ferrari turned up with six trucks, a motor-home and the Technogym transporter for the drivers to train in, plus... a staff of forty.

For its part, Toyota, on the eve of its debut at the big circus, was running simultaneously at two circuits. Mika Salo was driving at the new Paul Ricard track, while Allan McNish was hard at work in Barcelona. The Japanese company's test team boasts a staff of over one hundred people.

All the teams currently need a separate test squad and the freeing-up of the rules regarding testing means they are covering even greater distances than before. During the season, the front runners usually plan three days of testing in the week between Grands Prix. This was too much work for the race mechanics, hence the creation of the extra test team. Some racing teams employ test drivers, while others get their race drivers to do the work. In 2001, Ferrari did over 60,000 kilometres over the season between races and tests. McLaren have come up with even more precise statistics. In testing, Mika Häkkinen, David Coulthard and Alexander Wurz did 37,000 kilometres. Over the race weekends, the two drivers racked up 22,500 kilometres. Given the cost per kilometre, it is easy to see why the teams constantly need more money.

For several years now, Bernie Ecclestone and the FIA have proposed restrictions on testing, but a move to curb it down has failed. This winter, a long break was instigated to cut down costs. Right from the start of January, testing took off at such a pace that any money saved in December was spent. At the end of the 2002 season, testing will be allowed once again, but limited to 15 days per month. Another suggestion is doing the rounds. Why not organise additional Grands Prix and impose a complete ban on testing during the season? The wealthy teams, who are constantly looking to improve performance are not at all keen on the suggestion. The "little" teams will not be able to keep up with this pace for long. At the launch of his 2002 car, even Frank Williams admitted it was getting hard to dig out new sponsors. Everyone knows what Alain Prost thinks of it all. Even solid teams like Jordan are finding it tough going. In addition, the supply of cigarette money will run out in 2007. Renault, wishing to present a healthy image, had hoped to do without its Japanese cigarette money. But the company will still be "smoking" as it has not found a substitution benefactor. Who will replace the cigarette dollars which have kept Formula 1 alive these past thirty years? It had been thought that major food companies would rush to back the sport. We are still waiting. It is high time that the governing body tackles this problem which could kill the goose which laid the golden egg. If some of the teams disappear, a grid with only fifteen cars in unlikely to be attractive. Bernie Ecclestone has always preached in favour of quality rather than the quantity which existed in the old days of pre-qualifying. In 1989, there were thirty-nine names on the starting list for the Grands Prix. In 2002 there will be twenty-two. How many will there be in 2007?

Of course, there is always the possibility of letting the major manufacturers enter a third car. But with uniformity comes boredom. A championship staged with three red cars, three grey one, three white and three green may not be as appealing. The galloping inflation which has infected Formula 1 could cause serious damage. It is time to react before it is too late. Watch out! There is danger ahead. ∎

# DID YOU KNOW?

**The shortest circuit to host a Grand Prix?**
Long Beach (USA), in 1976 (2.220 km).

**The longest circuit to host a Grand Prix?**
Pescara (Italy), in 1957 (25.838 km).

**The longest distance for a Grand Prix?**
The Indy 500, in the 1950s (804.625 km) .

**The longest time for a Grand Prix?**
The 1951 Indy 500 (3 h 57' 38").

**The shortest time for a Grand Prix?**
The 1991 Australian GP, in Adelaide (24' 34.899).

**The shortest distance for a Grand Prix?**
The 1991 Australian GP, in Adelaide (53 km).

**The shortest distance for a Grand Prix in 2001?**
The Monaco GP (263.484 km).

**The longest distance for a Grand Prix in 2001?**
The Japanese GP, at Suzuka (310.476 km).

**The highest average speed for pole position?**
Keke Rosberg at Silverstone, in 1985 (258.984 kph).

**The highest average speed during a Grand Prix?**
Damon Hill at Monza, in 1993 (249.835 kph).

**The biggest gap between first and second at the end of a Grand Prix?**
2 laps at the 1969 Spanish Grand Prix (Jackie Stewart/ Bruce McLaren, and at the 1995 Australian Grand Prix (Damon Hill/Olivier Panis).

**The smallest gap between first and second at the end of a Grand Prix?**
1 hundredth of a second at the 1971 Italian GP (Peter Gethin/Ronnie Peterson).

**The greatest number of starters in a Grand Prix?**
34 at the 1953 German GP (Nürburgring).

**The smallest number of starters in a Grand Prix?**
13 at the 1968 Spanish GP (Jarama).

**The greatest number of finishers in a Grand Prix?**
22 at the 1952 British GP (Silverstone).

**The smallest number of finishers in a Grand Prix?**
4 at the 1966 Monaco GP.

**The circuit to have staged the most Grands Prix?**
Monza (51 times).

**The youngest driver to start a Grand Prix?**
Mike Thackwell (19 years and 182 days, 1980 Canadian GP).

**The oldest driver to start a Grand Prix?**
Louis Chiron (55, 1955 Monaco GP).

**The youngest driver to win a Grand Prix?**
Troy Ruttman (22, 1952 Indy 500).

**The oldest driver to win a Grand Prix?**
Luigi Fagioli (53, 1951 French GP).

**The youngest world champion?**
Emerson Fittipaldi (25 in 1972).

**The oldest world champion?**
Juan Manuel Fangio (46 in 1957).

**The greatest number of world titles by a driver?**
Juan-Manuel Fangio (5 times).

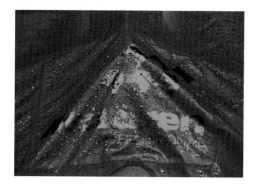

**The largest points gap between first and second place in the world championship?**
58 between Michael Schumacher and David Coulthard in 2001.

**The smallest points gap between first and second place in the world championship?**
Half a point between Niki Lauda and Alain Prost in 1984.

**The greatest number of Grand Prix starts?**
Riccardo Patrese (256).

**The greatest number of Grand Prix wins?**
Michael Schumacher (53).

**The greatest number of second places?**
Alain Prost (35).

**The greatest number of third places?**
Gerhard Berger (21).

**The greatest number of podiums?**
Alain Prost (106).

**The highest points total in a season?**
Michael Schumacher in 2001 (123).

**The highest points total in a driver's career?**
Michael Schumacher (801).

**The greatest number of wins in a season?**
Nigel Mansell in 1992, and Michael Schumacher in 1995, 2000 and 2001 (9).

**The greatest number of wins at the same Grand Prix?**
Ayrton Senna in Monaco, and Alain Prost in Brazil and France (6).

**The highest number of consecutive wins?**
Alberto Ascari over the 1952 and 1953 seasons (9)

**The highest number of kilometres in the lead?**
Michael Schumacher (14,318).

**The greatest number of pole positions?**
Ayrton Senna (65).

**The greatest number of consecutive pole positions?**
Ayrton Senna, 8 from the 1988 Spanish GP to the 1989 United States GP.

**The highest number of poles in one season?**
Nigel Mansell in 1992 (14).

**The highest number of fastest race laps?**
Michael Schumacher (44).

**The highest number of fastest race laps in one season?**
Nigel Mansell in 1992 (8).

**The greatest number of races led from start to finish by a driver?**
Ayrton Senna (19).

**The greatest number of wins by a country?**
187 wins, from 17 drivers for Great Britain.

**The highest number of wins by a constructor?**
Ferrari (144).

**The greatest number of titles by a constructor?**
Ferrari (11).

**The greatest number of pole positions by a constructor?**
Ferrari (148).

**The highest number of points by a constructor?**
Ferrari (2,692.5 points).

**The smallest number of wins in a season for the driver taking the world title?**
Mike Hawthorn in 1958, and Keke Rosberg in 1982 (1 win).

**The highest number of one-two finishes?**
Ferrari (47).

**The highest number of one-two finishes in one season?**
McLaren in 1988 (10).

**The greatest number of consecutive pole positions by a constructor?**
Williams, 24 from the 1992 French GP to the 1993 Japanese GP.

**The greatest number of poles in one season by a constructor?**
McLaren in 1988 and 1989, and Williams in 1992 and 1993 (15).

**The greatest number of consecutive wins by a constructor?**
Ferrari, 14 wins from the 1952 Swiss GP to the 1953 Swiss GP.

**The greatest number of wins at a circuit by a constructor?**
Ferrari at Monza (13).

**The highest number of wins by an engine manufacturer?**
Ford (175).

**The highest number of wins in one season by an engine manufacturer?**
Renault in 1995 (16).

**The greatest number of pole positions by an engine manufacturer?**
Renault in 1995 (16).

**The greatest number of wins by a tyre manufacturer?**
Goodyear (368).

**Which driver has raced for the most teams?**
Andrea de Cesaris (10 teams, from 1980 to 1994).

**Which driver holds the record for the highest number of consecutive wins in the same Grand Prix?**
Ayrton Senna (5 wins at Monaco, from 1989 to 1993).

**Which driver has finished the highest number of consecutive Grands Prix in the points?**
Carlos Reutemann (15 from the 1980 Belgian GP to the 1981 Belgian GP).

**Which driver has stayed with the same team for the longest time?**
Mika Häkkinen (8 full seasons - 132 GPs - for McLaren, from 1994 to 2001).

**Which drivers have been team-mates for the longest time?**
Mika Hakkinen and David Coulthard (6 seasons together at McLaren, from 1996 to 2001).

**Who scored the most lap records in 2001?**
Ralf Schumacher (5).

**Which driver has scored the highest points average per race in a season?**
Michael Schumacher (7.23 points, in 2001).

**What is the highest top speed ever recorded by a Formula 1 car?**
Jean Alesi's Jordan (363.2 kph at the 2001 Italian GP).

**The biggest accident in the history of Formula 1?**
The 1998 Belgian GP (13 cars involved).

# ORIGIN OF THE SPECIES

*Kerpen*

Starting last year, the blue riband world championship karting event, Formula Super A, was held over five rounds.

*Michael is always up for the traditional press conference.*

With the cancellation of the Japanese leg, the town of Kerpen in Germany, birthplace of the Schumacher brothers, put itself forward to organise the final round. Privately, the organisers hoped they would attract Michael Schumacher to attend the event. Their joy was complete when the four-times world champion decided to race. Jos Verstappen, Jarno Trulli, Kimi Räikkönen and Jenson Button were also trying to take part, but unfortunately they could not find a drive. Therefore, on October 28, 2001, the German driver was the only F1 standard bearer, up against the best young karters in the world. These eighteen-year-old youngsters race week after week and have total mastery of their machines. So, Schumacher's only advantage was his perfect knowledge of the track where he made his competition debut. Along with his friend Verstappen, he managed two testing sessions in Belgium in the weeks leading up to the race. Weight being the biggest handicap in karting, he had to lose four kilos to be in contention. In the first practice session, held on a greasy,

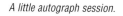

*A little autograph session.*

damp track, he set the best time in his group. Unfortunately for him, the track dried for runners in the other group. This meant he was only 23rd on the starting grid.

Despite this major handicap, the Ferrari driver took the bit between his teeth and in his first race, mounted a spectacular charge up through the field. Sadly, just as he had moved up to second place, a wheel bearing failed and he was forced to retire.

In the second leg, he managed to finish second, having put on an amazing performance.

Never one to turn down a challenge, Michael Schumacher had completed his mission. Of course, he had a good kart, which had been very well prepared, but nevertheless, it was a breathtaking performance. He took a hands-on role in preparing his machine, changing

Calm and relaxed, Michael heads for the grid.

His helmet was fitted with a special rotating device to clear the rain.

Michael shows everyone he is not afraid to rub shoulders with the young lions of the sport.

Michael Schumacher tries once more to fire up his kart, but in vain as the engine is broken.

his own engine, checking tyre pressures and generally doing all the race preparation work.

All through this damp October weekend, the four-times world champion made himself available to his fans. He seemed to enjoy their attention and genuinely took pleasure in going back to his racing roots. All the other competitors, most of them just kids, could not believe what was happening and the fact they could talk to and rub shoulders with one of the best drivers of all time. This back to basics approach, with Michael Schumacher humbly mucking in with the spirit of the event, meant he had written another page in his career history. Mad keen on cycling, he will probably try turning his hand to the world road racing championship next. Schumi's appetite for competition is really insatiable! ■

On a wet or dry track, Michael is still the man to beat.

Jordan Honda_Takuma Sato

Toyota_Allan McNish

Williams BMW_Juan Pablo Montoya

Ferrari_Rubens Barrichello

Sauber Petronas_Nick Heidfeld

Williams BMW_Juan Pablo Montoya

Renault_Jarno Trulli

# WHAT DO THEY DO NOW ?

*2002*

Since 1990, 103 drivers have taken part in at least one Formula One Grand Prix. Many of them have pursued other careers in motorsport after leaving the top level of racing. Others have done something completely different. Here is as precise a list as possible of what they are up to now. At this time of year, not all available drives in motor racing have been taken up and many of these former drivers are still waiting by the phone.

**A**

| | |
|---|---|
| Adams Philippe (2) | No longer racing |
| Alboreto Michele (194) | Killed in testing on April 25, 2001 |
| *Alesi Jean (201)* | *DTM (Mercedes)* |
| Alliot Philippe (109) | No longer racing |
| Alonso Fernando (17) | 3rd Renault driver |
| Andretti Michael (13) | CART |
| Apicella Marco (1) | No longer racing |

**B**

| | |
|---|---|
| Badoer Luca (51) | Ferrari F1 test driver |
| Bailey Julian (7) | No longer racing |
| Barbazza Fabrizio (8) | Businessman |
| Barilla Paolo (8) | Businessman |
| Barrichello Rubens (147) | Formula 1 (Ferrari) |
| Belmondo Paul (7) | GT (Viper) team owner |
| Beretta Olivier (10) | Endurance (Oreca) |
| Berger Gerhard (210) | BMW competition director |
| Bernard Eric (45) | Endurance (Cadillac) |
| Bernoldi Enrique (17) | Formula 1 (Arrows) |
| Blundell Mark (61) | No longer racing |
| Boullion Jean-Christophe(11) | Endurance |
| Boutsen Thierry (163) | Businessman |
| Brabham David (163) | Endurance (Panoz) |
| Brundle Martin (158) | TV Consultant |
| *Burti Luciano (15)* | *Ferrari F1 test driver* |
| Button Jenson (34) | Formula1 (Renault) |

**C**

| | |
|---|---|
| Caffi Alex (56) | Endurance |
| Capelli Ivan (93) | TV Consultant |
| Chiesa Andrea (3) | TV Consultant |
| Comas Erik (59) | Endurance |
| *Coulthard David (124)* | *Formula 1 (McLaren)* |

**D**

| | |
|---|---|
| *Dalmas Yannick (24)* | *Endurance* |
| De Cesaris Andrea (208) | Competitive wind surfing |
| De la Rosa Pedro (46) | Formula 1 (Arrows) |
| Deletraz Jean-Denis (3) | Endurance |
| Diniz Pedro (99) | Businessman |
| Donnelly Martin (14) | Businessman |

**E**

| | |
|---|---|
| Enge Tomas (3) | F 3000 (Arden) |

**F**

| | |
|---|---|
| Fisichella Giancarlo (91) | Formula 1 (Jordan) |
| *Fittipaldi Christian (40)* | *CART (Newman Haas)* |
| Foitek Gregor (7) | No longer racing |
| Fontana Norberto (4) | Touring cars in Argentina |
| Frentzen Heinz-Harald (129) | Formula 1 (Arrows) |

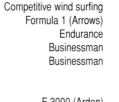

**G**

| | |
|---|---|
| Gachot Bernard (47) | Businessman |
| Giacomelli Bruno (69) | No longer racing |
| Gounon Jean-Marc (9) | Endurance |
| Grouillard Olivier (41) | Touring cars in France |
| Gugelmin Maurizio (74) | No longer racing |

**H**

| | |
|---|---|
| Häkkinen Mika (162) | Sabbatical year |
| Heidfeld Nick (34) | Formula 1 (Sauber) |
| Herbert Johnny (162) | Endurance (Audi) |
| **Hill Damon (116)** | **Various business interests** |

**I**

| | |
|---|---|
| Inoue Taki (18) | No longer racing |
| Irvine Eddie (130) | Formula 1 (Jaguar) |

**J**

| | |
|---|---|
| **Johansson Stefan (79)** | **Endurance (Ferrari & Audi)** |

**K**

| | |
|---|---|
| Katayama Ukyo (95) | No longer racing |

**L**

| | |
|---|---|
| Lagorce Franck (2) | Endurance (Pescarolo) |
| Lammers Jan (23) | Endurance (Audi) |
| Lamy Pedro (32) | GT in Australia (Ford) |
| Larini Nicola (49) | Touring cars (Alfa Romeo) |
| Lavaggi Giovanni (7) | Businessman |
| Lehto Jyrky (62) | Endurance (Cadillac) |

**M**

| | |
|---|---|
| Mansell Nigel (187) | Golf club owner |
| Magnussen Jan (24) | Endurance (Panoz) |
| Marques Tarso (26) | No longer racing |
| Martini Pierluigi (119) | Businessman |
| Mazzacane Gaston (21) | No longer racing |
| Modena Stefano (70) | Businessman |
| Montermini Andrea (21) | TV Consultant |
| Montoya Juan Pablo (17) | Formula 1 (Williams) |
| Morbidelli Gianni (67) | No longer racing |
| Moreno Roberto (42) | No longer racing |

**N**

| | |
|---|---|
| Nakajima Satoru (74) | F3 and F3000 team owner in Japan |
| Nakano Shinji (33) | CART (Fernandez) |
| Nannini Alessandro (77) | Businessman |
| Naspetti Emanuele (5) | Endurance (Ferrari) |
| Noda Hideki (3) | IRL |

**P**

| | |
|---|---|
| Panis Olivier (108) | Formula 1 (BAR) |
| Papis Massimo (7) | CART (Sigma) and endurance (Dallara) |
| **Patrese Ricardo (256)** | **Businessman** |
| **Piquet Nelson (204)** | **In business & looking after the career of his son Nelsinho** |
| Pirro Emanuele (37) | Endurance (Audi) |
| Prost Alain (199) | Out of work since Prost GP went bankrupt |

**R**

| | |
|---|---|
| Räikkönen Kimi (17) | Formula 1 (McLaren) |
| Ratzenberger Roland (1) | Killed at Imola on April 30, 1994 |
| Rosset Ricardo (32) | Businessman |

**S**

| | |
|---|---|
| Salo Mika (95) | Formula 1 (Toyota) |
| Sarrazin Stéphane (1) | No longer racing |
| Schiatarella Domenico (6) | Endurance (Ferrari) |
| Schneider Bernd (9) | DTM (Mercedes) |
| Schumacher Michael (162) | Formula 1 (Ferrari) |
| Schumacher Ralf (83) | Formula 1 (Williams) |
| Senna Ayrton (161) | Killed at Imola on May 1, 1994 |
| Suzuki Aguri (64) | F3 and F3000 team owner in Japan |

**T**

| | |
|---|---|
| Takagi Toranosuke (32) | CART |
| Tarquini Gabriele (38) | Touring cars |
| Tuero Esteban (16) | Touring cars in Argentina (VW) |
| Trulli Jarno (80) | Formula 1 (Renault) |

**V**

| | |
|---|---|
| Van de Poele Eric (5) | Endurance (Bentley) |
| Verstappen Jos (91) | No longer racing |
| Villeneuve Jacques (99) | Formula 1 (BAR) |

**W**

| | |
|---|---|
| Warwick Derek (147) | Businessman |
| Wendlinger Karl (41) | Endurance |
| **Wurz Alexander (52)** | **3rd driver for McLaren in F1** |

**Y**

| | |
|---|---|
| Yoong Alex (3) | Formula 1 (Minardi) |

**Z**

| | |
|---|---|
| Zanardi Alex (41) | No longer racing |
| **Zonta Ricardo (31)** | **No longer racing** |

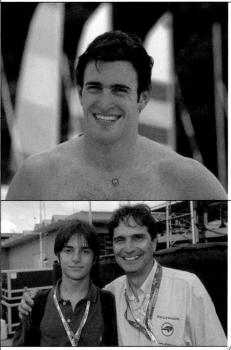

# PROST

*Grand Prix*

On Monday January 28, 2002, the Commercial Tribunal of Versailles declared that the Prost Grand Prix team was officially bankrupt. This decision was not really a surprise, because the only French F1 team had been dying a slow death. After the courts had taken over the team on November 22, 2001, there was no rush of investors keen to take over the team.

*Jacques Calvet with Alain Prost in 1997*

With debts of 30 million Euros, the team was no longer an attractive proposition. Right at the start of a recession, after the events of September 11, a lot of investments had been frozen. In these circumstances, the team's situation seemed hopeless and it was not enough to make an offer to Alain Prost, who had stood alongside his troops right to the bitter end. His difficult personality definitely did not help matters, when it came to finding a solution to the problem. The champion driver, famous the world over, had evoked feelings of jealousy in several quarters and there were many former colleagues who gathered like vultures around the mortally wounded animal.

This brilliant champion soon realised that running a large company was not a trifling matter. You cannot control it in the way you can dominate other drivers on the track. Several personalities from the world of motor racing did not hold back in spitting their venom at the greatest French driver in history, revealing old and bitter feuds. One thing is for sure; not everyone in the sport was his friend. His strong personality and introverted character sometimes worked against him throughout his long racing career. He often had a tendency to portray himself as a hard-done-by martyr. It is not always a good thing to speak one's mind or tell the truth. Throughout his long and exceptional career in Formula 1, he was never able to hide his feelings or his state of mind. Having clashed with his team-mate Rene Arnoux and boss Gerard Larrousse at Renault, he went to war with Ayrton Senna at McLaren. Later he was sacked from

Ferrari after airing his opinions on the Scuderia too publicly.

When it came to running his own team, he was captain of the ship and found it hard to delegate.

No doubt that failing contributed to the demise of his team. Even though he defends his actions, he refused to hand over the rudder to save the team, preferring to go down with his ship.

2001: Alain Prost with Pelé and Pedro Diniz at the Brazilian Grand Prix.

The association with Pedro Diniz could have set the team on an even keel again at the end of 2000. This was the great white hope for quite some time, but the worm was already in the apple. Throughout its life, Prost Grand Prix suffered from a lack of stability. The move from Magny-Cours to Guyancourt could have been delayed. Instead, the workforce and their families were thrown off-guard, landing in the unprepossessing Parisian suburb, when they had been used to the peace and tranquility of the countryside. Over the course of five seasons, well respected technical directors came and went, without coming up with the miracle solution. The constant change of engine supplier did not help the situation either. Even on the driver front there were problems. No less than eight of them wore the blue of Prost. After Olivier Panis, a veritable institution for the "Blues", came Jean Alesi, who despite being a friend of the boss, threw in the towel before his time was up, at his wits end with all the in-fighting. Feeling he was getting unfair treatment, Prost's relations with the press were often stormy. He sometimes thinks the whole world is against him. It is almost a persecution complex. The sponsors were not really given the red carpet treatment; something the English teams do so well. One by one they left and were never replaced. Poor results did not make it easy to find new ones. The infernal downward spiral was taking its toll. In a sport where money is the only currency, the die was cast. In France, businesses operate under a vast number of restrictions. Going for patriotism, Alain Prost refused to move his team to England, where tax and employment laws are more relaxed. It has to be said that the amounts paid to the French inland revenue over this period certainly contributed to putting the team out of business. But what a waste! It was all too good to be true. The greatest French champion had bought Ligier, the only French team which could let Prost realise his dream of glory. "We are aiming at the world championship title in three years," claimed Alain Prost. Sponsors flocked to get on the bandwagon. The first results did not take long to come. Right from the start of the 1997 season, Olivier Panis was on brilliant form. A few months later, his accident in Montreal knocked the stuffing out of the team. Jarno Trulli stood in until the French driver was back in harness.

Despite everything, the first year had gone well, resulting in sixth place in the championship. The switch to Peugeot did not go smoothly as the engines lacked power and were unreliable. A slight resurgence in 1999 was followed by another catastrophic season, with not a single point scored. Prost and Peugeot went through the inevitable divorce and that was the beginning of the end for the French team.

The Prost team's fate was sealed in 2000. With no money in the kitty, Prost paid through the nose to hire Ferrari engines. Jean Alesi brought some hope in the shape of a few points, before slamming the door shut behind him just before the race at Hockenheim. No one was surprised.

After Jack Brabham, John Surtees, Graham Hill, Emerson Fittipaldi and Jackie Stewart, all of them world champions and owners of their own teams, Alain Prost suffered the same fate as his illustrious companions. Jackie Stewart alone had the good sense to sell his team, pulling off a great deal before it was too late. But, on the day his team went under, Alain Prost was keen to reassure his numerous supporters that he would bounce back, one way or another. ■

### Prost Grand Prix – The statistics

83 grands prix entered.
35 points scored.
Best results: two second places: Spain 1997 (Panis) and Europe 1999 (Trulli).
Best classification in the Constructors' World Championship: 6th in 1997.
1997: 6th, 21 points.
1998: 9th, 1 point.
1999: 7th, 9 points.
2000: not classified, 0 points.
2001: 9th, 4 points.

### Prost Grand Prix drivers

1997: Olivier Panis, Shinji Nakano and Jarno Trulli.
1998: Olivier Panis and Jarno Trulli.
1999: Olivier Panis and Jarno Trulli.
2000: Jean Alesi and Nick Heidfeld.
2001: Jean Alesi, Gaston Mazzacane, Luciano Burti and Tomas Enge.

# KEN**TYRRELL**

*Last of the Giants*

One of the last living legends of motorsport passed away on 25th August 2001. He died just a few months after another colossus of Formula 1; his friend John Cooper, who played a part in his debut in the blue riband of motor racing.

Piles of cash do not make history. Grand Prix legends were written by a handful of pioneers who revolutionised the modern era of motor racing. At the end of the Seventies, Formula 1 became the victim of its own success and more and more money was needed to challenge the major car manufacturers who were just discovering the attractions of the sport. Artisans like Lotus, Brabham and Tyrrell could no longer match the resources of the motor industry giants. They were unable to evolve or take the necessary leap forward.

It was Ken Tyrrell who held out the longest, in the face of this unequal opposition, as the other great names gradually disappeared from the scene. The former timber merchant turned team owner would be the last of the dinosaurs. Financial pressures eventually took their toll at the end of the '97 season.

Ken Tyrrell really left his mark on the sport. His sense of organisation, tactical ability and the way he ran his team served as a model for others who followed. His professional approach revolutionised the world of motor racing.

There was another area where Tyrrell excelled and that was in spotting young talent. In 1964, he took on a young and inexperienced driver called Jackie Stewart, who would go on to be one of the all-time greats. The Scottish driver would bring the Tyrrell team its greatest successes.

Their Formula 1 partnership ran for six years from 1968 to 1973. They won three Drivers' World Championships and one Constructors' trophy.

In fact, Tyrrell's team was one big family. He was always paternal and friendly towards his drivers. Without a doubt, Jackie Stewart is best placed to talk about his former boss, with whom he was very close. *"Along with my family, Ken Tyrrell was the most important person in my life. He was like a father to me, but much more than that and more than a manager. Without him, I would not be the man I am today. "Tyrrell Racing Organisation" was a real family. In its day, it was quite simply the best and Ken was a unique person. We will never see the like of him again in Formula 1."*

Francois Cevert, Patrick Depailler, Jody Scheckter, Didier Pironi, Michele Alboreto, Stefan Bellof and Jean Alesi are just some of the numerous drivers discovered by this talented man and they carried the Tyrrell colours to success over 30 years in Formula 1. ∎

*Matra' Story: the championship winning MS80, seen here, evolving at the 1969 South African GP.*

Here is a timeline of the life of Ken Tyrrell:

**1924:** Robert Kenneth Tyrrell is born in West Horsley, in Surrey, to the south west of London on 3rd May.

**1943:** He marries Norah on 15th June. They have two sons, one of them, Bob, went on to work for Team Tyrrell.

**1944:** Ken Tyrrell joins the Royal Air Force.

**1947:** Along with his brother, he sets up a timber business.

**1951:** On an outing organised by his football club, he attends the Daily Express Trophy, a non-championship Formula 1 race, held at Silverstone over the Easter weekend. It was his first taste of motor racing and that day changed his life.

**1952:** Ken Tyrrell makes his racing debut at Snetterton, at the wheel of a Formula 3 Cooper.

**1953:** Ken Tyrrell takes his first wins in F3 at Snetterton and Kirkaldy, as well as picking up several podium finishes.

**1954:** He becomes Irish Formula 3 champion and wins an international event at Karlskoga in Sweden.

**1958:** Still faithful to the Cooper marque, he decides to move up to Formula 2, after teaming up with Alan Brown and Cecil Libowicz. Tyrrell soon realises that he does not have the talent to take him to the top. He makes the logical decision to hang up his helmet and move into management.

**1959:** John Cooper entrusts him with the running of his Formula 2 team, running Bruce McLaren, Jack Brabham and Masten Gregory.

**1960:** He sets up his own organisation, called the "Ken Tyrrell Racing Team." He runs the works Coopers in Formula Junior. One of his drivers wins the prestigious Monaco race.

**1962:** His drivers, Tony Maggs and John Love completely dominate the Formula Junior championship.

**1963:** While returning home from testing a double engined Mini which he had built, John Cooper has an accident and hands over the running of his Formula 1 team to Ken Tyrrell. In the space of a few short months, Ken shows his management ability and mastery of tactics. The image of cunning Ken is born.

**1964:** Back in the lower formulae, he puts a young man called Jackie Stewart in one of his Cooper T72 Formula 3 cars. The Scotsman dominates the series. In 1965, as newly-crowned British F3 champion, Stewart gets an F1 drive with BRM. At the same time, he continues to drive in F2 in a Cooper, managed by Tyrrell.

**1966:** The Tyrrell organisation runs Matra-BRMs in Formula 2. Tyrrell has spotted and signed up a promising young Belgian, Jacky Ickx. The team is now called "Tyrrell Racing Organisation."

**1967:** Ickx makes the most of the opportunity. He wins the European F2 Trophy in a Matra MS7-Cosworth. The Tyrrell team no longer has anything to prove in this category.

Ken Tyrrell prepares to take the step up into Formula 1, along with his French partner Matra.

**1968:** Jackie Stewart leaves BRM to return to his mentor. Along with Jean-Pierre Beltoise he gives the new Matra-Elf its F1 debut. Tyrrell does a great job of running the team and has also brought along the new Ford Cosworth DFV engine.

Right from the very first year, Stewart wins three races in Holland, Germany and the United States and even poses a threat to eventual championship winner, Graham Hill in the Lotus.

**1969:** Jackie Stewart is unwilling to settle for the odd victory. He completely dominates the championship, taking six wins. Matra is also world champion thanks to the efficiency of the Tyrrell organisation. However, this successful partnership would not last long. The French company wants to race its V12 engine and Ken Tyrrell plans to continue with the Ford Cosworth unit. The

Ken Tyrrell and Jackie Stewart were very close.

Jackie Stewart and Francois Cevert score an historic one - two at the 1971 German GP.

Monaco 1970

divorce comes through at the end of this successful year.

**1970:** Tyrrell switches to a chassis from a new company called March. Jackie Stewart is still with the team. He is partnered by Johnny Servoz-Gavin and then by Francois Cevert. However, the Ford-powered March is not up to the job. Once the season is underway, Tyrrell decides to join forces with a former Ferguson engineer, Derek Gardner, to build his own car in a corner of the Tyrrell Bros timber yard, in Ockham. The Tyrrell 001 makes its debut at the Canadian Grand Prix. This brand new car will give Tyrrell the chance to return to his winning ways.

**1971:** Well supported by Francois Cevert, who wins the United States Grand Prix, Jackie Stewart wins five Grands Prix, to take his second world title. "Elf Team Tyrrell" are the boys to beat and the benchmark in Formula 1. Ken Tyrrell can afford a toothy grin. He has won his bet.

**1972:** The Tyrrells of Stewart and Cevert are unable to hinder the unstoppable Emerson Fittipaldi, who becomes the youngest ever world champion in his black and gold liveried JPS Lotus.

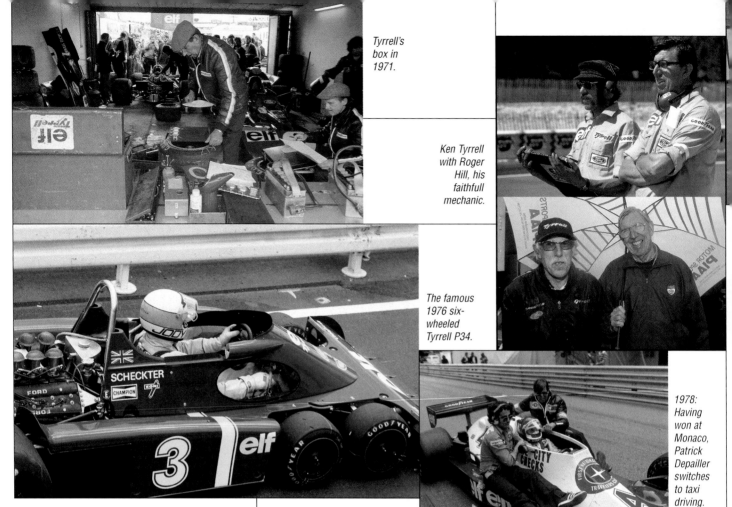

*Tyrrell's box in 1971.*

*Ken Tyrrell with Roger Hill, his faithfull mechanic.*

*The famous 1976 six-wheeled Tyrrell P34.*

*1978: Having won at Monaco, Patrick Depailler switches to taxi driving.*

**1973:** The odd-numbered years seem to suit Tyrrell. The new 006, still fitted with the Ford Cosworth engine, takes the team's favourite driver, Jackie Stewart, to a third title. Big Ken's blue cars are untouchable. The Scotsman wins five times, three of them ahead of team-mate Francois Cevert.

Tragically, the Frenchman is killed during practice for the United States Grand Prix. A traumatised Jackie Stewart retires on the spot. He has 27 victories to his name, beating Jim Clark's previous record of 25. It is the end of an era.

**1974:** Still with backing from French oil company Elf, Ken Tyrrell is forced to rebuild his team. He takes on Patrick Depailler, who had made his debut with the team back in the 1972 French Grand Prix and South African Jody Scheckter, who had made a name for himself the previous year, in a McLaren.

Scheckter takes two wins and the team is third in the Constructors' Championship.

**1975:** Jody Scheckter kicks off the season by winning his home Grand Prix. Sadly, it would be his only success of the season. Tyrrells are often front runners, but never take the top slot.

**1976:** Designer Derek Gardner rolls up his sleeves. He comes up with a crazy car, the P34, fitted with four small steering front wheels. It creates enormous media interest. Fine tuning this revolutionary car proves difficult. Despite that, Scheckter and Depailler pull off a fantastic one-two in Sweden with this car. While it picked

*Detroit 1983: Michele Alboreto takes Tyrrell's 23rd and final Grand Prix win.*

up the points, it never won again. The four front wheel concept would be taken up again by Williams and Ferrari, who tried it in practice, with a different concept for the rear end of their cars.

**1977:** Jody Scheckter moves to Wolf and is replaced by the Swede, Ronnie Peterson. He and Depailler discover that the heavy six-wheeled Tyrrell is not a winning machine. Tyrrell sinks into the pack and the car's designer Derek Gardner is replaced by Maurice Philippe, who opts for more conventional solutions.

**1978:** Patrick Depailler wins the Monaco Grand Prix with the Tyrrell 008. But further wins will be few and far between. In fact, Tyrrell will wait four years to see one of his drivers on the top step of the podium.

**1982:** Using his knack at spotting new talent, Tyrrell signs up a young Italian F3 driver, Michele Alboreto. The move would put the smile back on "Uncle Ken's" face. In Las Vegas, he wins the jackpot. Turbocharged engines have arrived in force on the grid, but Tyrrell fights the change, being opposed to this technology.

One of the old school of artisans takes his revenge with the venerable Ford Cosworth, which is now out-paced on the track.

**1983:** Once again, thanks to Michele Alboreto, the Tyrrell team takes its last ever Grand Prix win, in Detroit. The infernal downward spiral is about to get underway. The lack of success makes it hard for Tyrrell to find backers to climb back up the grid. The famous Okham squad is losing its appeal.

**1984:** Handicapped by a Ford engine which is giving away horsepower to the turbo motors and their huge power output, Ken Tyrrell refuse to give up the fight. He takes on two young hopefuls; Englishman Martin Brundle and Germany's Stefan Bellof.

Unable to fight on equal terms, Ken Tyrrell's cunning catches him out. His team is excluded from the season's results after it is found to have cheated. In order to close the performance gap, he builds his cars under the legal minimum weight limit. Before scrutineering, a team mechanic would fill the car with fuel, loaded up with led ball bearings, to reach the minimum weight. The revelation caused a lot of fuss in the paddock. It was a

*An image which has entered the pages of F1 history: Jean Alesi leads the United States GP at Phoenix, ahead of Ayrton Senna.*

**1991:** The arrival of the Honda engine and Stefano Modena allows Tyrrell to save face and the team finishes sixth in the Constructors' Championship.

**1992:** With Andrea De Cesaris and Olivier Grouillard, Tyrrell treads water. Despite some honourable results, the team finds it harder and harder to attract sponsors. He no longer has a big enough budget to move forward. Gradually, the team sinks into anonymity. The Tyrrells are just there to make up the numbers, occasionally picking up a point or two. During this time, Bernie Ecclestone bails the team out on several occasions, to save what is an institution in peril.

**1997:** On 7th December, after another lacklustre season, Ken Tyrrell throws in the towel. He is forced to sell his team to British American Tobacco, who are about to enter the F1 arena. It's the end of an era and an incredible story.

**1998:** The legendary Tyrrell name is still to be found on the nose of the white cars bought by BAR. But old Ken is no longer at the helm. His distinctive frame is no longer seen in the paddock. Whether it is a coincidence or not, the British American Racing Tyrrells fail to score a single point all year. It might have brought a sneaky smile to the face of the wise old man, the patriarch of F1. But now he has a bigger battle on his hands, fighting off serious illness, which he does with determination and courage.

*Hungarian GP 2000: Ken Tyrrell with the pillars of the young BAR team, Craig Pollock and Jacques Villeneuve.*

**1999:** Having recovered from a successful operation to remove a tumour, he and wife Nora are occasional visitors to the F1 paddock.

**2001:** On 25th August, Ken Tyrrell dies of cancer of the pancreas. ■

desperate move by a team which was on its uppers.

**1985:** Ken Tyrrell fights back, finally switching to power from Renault, which he had strongly objected to at the end of the 70s. His season is marred by the death of his number one driver, Stefan Bellof, killed during an endurance race at Spa, when he collided with Jacky Ickx.

**1989:** Having gone through another bad patch, when the Tyrrell team lost direction, the team boss decided to dispose of the services of Michele Alboreto, who had returned to the team, replacing him at the French Grand Prix with a young Frenchman. Jean Alesi finished fourth on his Formula 1 debut.

**1990:** This year is in many ways Ken Tyrrell's swan song. The technical team come up with the idea of a raised nose, which is the sensation of the season and is still in vogue today. Jean Claude Migeot was the father of this design. *"This Tyrrell 019 is a real missile,"* enthuses Jean Alesi. He pulls off some remarkable performances in the car. In Phoenix he has a terrific duel with Ayrton Senna, going on to finish a brilliant second. He does the same in Monaco. With some other good results, the Tyrrell team finished fifth in the Constructors' Championship.

## *Tyrrell Team Statistics from 1968 to 1998*

441 grands prix contested
16 pole positions
32 wins
30 fastest race laps
1 Constructors' World Championship in 1971
3 Drivers' World Championships in 1969, 1971 and 1973 with Jackie Stewart
Twice runner-up in the Constructors' World Championship in 1972 and 1973
564 points scored.

**KEN TYRRELL'S DRIVERS:**

From 1968 to 1998, here is the list of the 39 drivers who raced for Ken Tyrrell:
Jackie Stewart: (1968 to 1973), 70 GPs
Johnny Servoz-Gavin: (1968 to 1970), 10 GPs
Jean-Pierre Beltoise: (1968 to 1969), 23 GPs
François Cevert: (1970 to 1973), 46 GPs
Peter Revson: (USA 1971), 1 GP
Patrick Depailler: (France and USA 1972, and then 1974 to 1978), 80 GPs
Chris Amon: (Canada and USA 1973), 2 GPs
Jody Scheckter: (1974 to 1976), 45 GPs

Jean-Pierre Jabouille: (France 1975), 1 GP
Michel Leclère: (USA 1975), 1 GP
Ronnie Peterson: (1977), 17 GPs
Didier Pironi: (1978 to 1979), 31 GPs
Jean-Pierre Jarier: (1979 to 1980), 27 GPs
Derek Daly: (Austria 1979 and season 1980), 16 GPs
Geoff Lees: (Germany 1979), 1 GP
Mike Thackwell: (Canada and USA-East 1980, Germany 1984), 3 GPs
Eddie Cheever: (1981), 14 GPs
Michele Alboreto: (1981 to 1983, Brazil to Canada 1989), 46 GPs
Slim Borgudd: (South-Africa to USA-West 1982), 3 GPs
Brian Henton: (San Marino to Las Vegas 1982), 13 GPs
Danny Sullivan: (1983), 15 GPs
Martin Brundle: (1984 to 1986), 38 GPs
Stefan Bellof: (1984 to Holland 1985), 20 GPs
Stefan Johansson: (Britain to Holland 1984 and Brazil 1985), 4 GPs
Ivan Capelli: (Europe and Australia 1985), 2 GPs
Philippe Streiff: (South-Africa 1985, 1986 to 1987), 33 GPs
Jonathan Palmer: (1987 to 1989), 45 GPs
Julian Bailey: (1988), 6 GPs
Jean Alesi: (France to Australia 1989, except Belgium and

Portugal and season 1990), 23 GPs
Johnny Herbert: (Belgium and Portugal 1989), 2 GPs
Satoru Nakajima: (1990 to 1991), 31 GPs
Stefano Modena: (1991), 16 GPs
Olivier Grouillard: (1992), 16 GPs
Andrea De Cesaris: (1992 to 1993), 32 GPs
Ukyo Katayama: (1993 to 1996), 64 GPs
Mark Blundell: (1994), 16 GPs
Mika Salo: (1995 to 1997), 50 GPs
Gabriele Tarquini: (Europe 1995), 1 GP
Jos Verstappen: (1997), 17 GPs
Ricardo Rosset: (1998), 16 GPs
Toranosuke Takagi: (1998), 16 GPs

Author's note: From 1973 to 1977, privately entered Tyrrells occasionally raced in the hands of: Eddie Keizan, Ian Scheckter, Alessandro Pesanti-Rossi, Otto Stuppacher, Kazuyoshi Hoshino and Kinimitsu Takahaschi.

In 1998, the Tyrrell team was bought by BAR, but for its final year, it retained its legendary name. However, Ken Tyrrell was no longer in charge.

# BENETTON

*The Colourful side of Formula 1*

Thanks to a new technology for working with wool, the Benetton brothers, from Treviso in Italy, made a fortune in ready-to-wear clothes in the Seventies.

*The debut as title sponsor with Toleman.*

A palette full of new colours and new designs were all the rage with the younger generation. Benetton shops sprung up on every high street and did amazing business. Luciano Benetton was well aware of the value of publicity and it did not take him long to spot the enormous appeal of Formula 1. In 1983, he made the most of Ken Tyrrell's money worries and the presence in the team of Italian driver Michele Alboreto, to dip his toe in the water. The cars were painted in the green and yellow colours of the Italian company. Luciano Benetton wanted to branch out into the lucrative American market. He even pushed the team into taking on the American driver, Danny Sullivan. Alboreto's victory in Detroit could not have come at a better time. But despite this startling result, the rest of the season was disappointing. He therefore decided to switch his efforts to Alfa Romeo for 1984, but the Italian car manufacturer's team was not a success. At the end of 1985, the Benetton team switched tactics. It bought the Toleman team, which had given Ayrton Senna his first Formula 1 drive in 1984. The new team was called Benetton Formula Limited. Thanks to his connections, Luciano Benetton managed to get a supply of engines from BMW. In 1986, Teo Fabi and Gerhard Berger were the new team's first drivers. The livery of the B 186

reflects the Treviso company's marketing philosophy, with vibrant colours dominating. It's a revolution in Formula 1. The team kit consists of green trousers and pink shirts and then engine cover is a veritable kaleidoscope of colour. In Detroit, even the Benettons' tyres are painted pink, green and blue. In the pits, the mechanics work to the sound of rock music blaring in the garage.

The company motto, "United Colours of Benetton" is the cornerstone of this young and dynamic team. On top of that, the results start to roll in. In the very first year, Gerhard Berger wins the Mexican Grand Prix to give the sweater company its first taste of victory.

*United Colours right down to the tyre walls.*

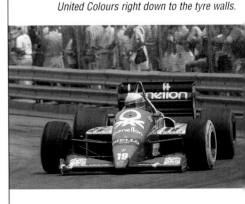

Monaco 1986

Holland 1984

The first win with Gerhard Berger in the 1986 Mexican GP.

To replace departing BMW, Benetton hitches its wagon to Ford engines, but Thierry Boutsen and Alessandro Nannini are unable to deliver the right sort of results. Reliability is not good and wrecks the team's chances. It was not until the very end of the season and the disqualification of Ayrton Senna and Japan, that Alessandro Nannini gave the team its next victory. To get the team back on track again, Luciano Benetton appointed his own choice of team leader at the end of 1988. The man was unknown in Formula 1, but he held the team's destiny in his hands. His name was Flavio Briatore. He would inject dynamism into the team and bring a new dimension to Benetton. In his opinion, a relaxed atmosphere and good communication are the key ingredients. Shortly after taking over, he contracted double world champion, Nelson Piquet to drive for the team in 1990.

The young and relaxed atmosphere in the squad brought the best out of the Brazilian, who enjoyed an exceptional year. The fact that he was paid per point scored proved to be a great motivator. With metronomic regularity, he racked up 43 points and won the last two Grands Prix of the season. His team-mate, Alessandro Nannini also played his part, until a dramatic helicopter crash ended his career. The two men took Benetton to third place in the Constructors' World Championship. Strongly recommended by Nelson Piquet, Roberto Moreno was brought in to replace the unfortunate Nannini and even finished second behind his friend in Japan.

The Anglo-Italian squad was now a member of the

exclusive "top team" club. The contrast with the austerity and lack of imagination that reigned in the other teams was marked. Benetton never passed up the opportunity to celebrate and party. Briatore was a firm believer in never taking oneself too seriously.

In 1991, with the arrival of a sack of gold from Camel cigarettes, the cars changed from their traditional green to yellow. Piquet and Moreno were not able to fight for the top places, although Piquet salvaged a win when Mansell retired at the last corner of the Canadian Grand Prix.

The sensational debut performance of Michael Schumacher would overturn the team's future. Flavio Briatore pulled off the ultimate midnight rain, snatching the young German prodigy from the grasp of Eddie Jordan. From the very next race at Monza, he replaced Moreno, who was unceremoniously dumped, and finished a strong fifth. The day before, Nelson Piquet had celebrated the fact he would be starting his 200th Grand Prix in a tense atmosphere. The presence of Schumacher was already putting him in the shade. He knew his days at Benetton were numbered and had already had a stormy meeting with Briatore.

In 1992, Michael Schumacher motivates the team. He takes his first win at Spa and with Martin Brundle, sets the team back on the road to success. The following year, with Ricardo Patrese, Benetton is once again third in the Constructors' Championship.

Michael Schumacher is in the ascendant and starts to put the Williams team and even Ayrton Senna under

From 1987 to 1990, the Benetton team proudly displayed the company colours.

The 1989 weaponry: Johnny Herbert, Alessandro Nannini and the B189.

From 1989 to 1995, Benetton made constant progress.

1991: Michael Schumacher makes his debut in Belgium with Jordan, but by the next GP, he was driving for Benetton. It was a shrewd move…

1990 Japanese GP: an incredible one-two with Nelson Piquet and Roberto Moreno.

…One year later, again in Belgium, he won his first GP ahead of Nigel Mansell and Riccardo Patrese.

circumstances, after a coming together with his only rival, Damon Hill. There were extraordinary scenes as the German returned to the pits. Schumacher and Briatore were overjoyed and they had grown close throughout the season. After every win, the driver would jump into his boss' arms with a demonstration of happiness which was guaranteed to upset his rivals. Benetton is carving a name for itself. Throughout the year, Briatore and his efficient marketing and PR operation never miss a chance to put on a publicity stunt in the paddock. It is an effective campaign. Models, dressed in team colours are an excellent way of promoting the brand: table football, table tennis, darts, rodeo riding, tennis tournaments and football matches are all organised to entertain the press.

The night of the championship in Adelaide, the team organised a huge party, inviting the entire paddock to free drinks. That night the whisky and beer flowed like water.

Luciano Benetton had won his bet. His name was now forever engraved in the F1 history books. Having taken the drivers' title, he would now rely on the effectiveness of Briatore and the skill of Schumacher to take both drivers' and constructors' titles.

pressure. He wins again in Portugal and finishes fourth in the world championship.

In 1994, the Japanese tobacco brand, Mild Seven comes on board and once again the team changes colour, turning to blue, while staying faithful to Ford engines. Michael Schumacher proves untouchable, even before the tragic loss of Ayrton Senna and then he dominates Damon Hill. He also has to put up with a two-race ban and two disqualifications for technical infringements. Nevertheless, he wins eight times and takes the title at the final round in Adelaide, in pathetic

1991 Canadian GP: Nelson Piquet takes his last win.

Nelson Piquet's 200th Grand Prix- something to celebrate.

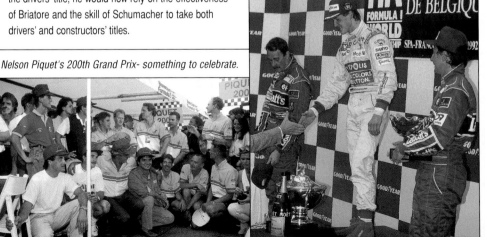

Brazil 1993

Michael Schumacher, Flavio Briatore and Luciano Benetton.

*Monaco 1994: first victory in the Principality.*

*Adelaide 1994 and Aïda 1995, the final consecration.*

*1994-1995: the team is on top of its game, with 18 wins, two drivers' and one constructors' title. The dream team has now switched to Ferrari: Michael Schumacher, Ross Brawn and Rory Byrne.*

In 1995, Michael Schumacher and his Benetton had a Renault engine and that meant they could challenge Williams on level terms. Schumacher did not wait to the end of the year: at the Pacific Grand Prix in Japan, he took his second title as well as bringing the team the constructors' crown. It had been a total success. In less than ten years, this young team had managed to drag itself to the top of the heap. Michael Schumacher had been the catalyst. His presence in the outfit let one think that Benetton could be a dominant force, establishing a hegemony in F1.

But that ignores the fact that the German likes a challenge. Despite his close links to the team, he could not resist the siren call of Ferrari; every driver's dream. The Benetton team would never recover from his departure. The arrival of Jean Alesi and Gerhard Berger was not enough to fill the gap he left behind. Lack of motivation certainly had something to do with it. Despite ten podium finishes and a third place in the constructors' championship, the spring had snapped. Minor places replaced victories. It is hard to get to the top, but even harder to stay there. The Benetton team followed the cruel example of several others before them. Leaving a sinking ship, Ross Brawn and Rory Byrne, the two technical bosses followed Schumacher to Ferrari at the end of 1996.

The team did reasonably well the following year, but it had lost its shine. The colours of Benetton were fading

and lacked sparkle. All the same, Gerhard Berger managed to win the German Grand Prix. It would be Benetton's last ever Formula 1 victory.

Flavio Briatore also suffered and seemed to lose his way during this time and also quit at the end of the year, worn out by the strain of it all. He was replaced by David Richards, an interloper from the world of rallying.

In 1998, the team slumped still further, despite the arrival of two young, talented, but inexperienced drivers, Giancarlo Fisichella and Alex Wurz. It slid into the anonymity of the pack. David Richards left, unhappy at the interference of the Benetton family. They replaced him with Rocco, Luciano Benetton's younger brother. There was good cause to be sceptical about the team's future. The young man was full of good intentions, but had absolutely no experience of motorsport. He was put in charge of a team struggling to come up for air. He could not work miracles and podiums were few and far between.

The team was now firmly fixed in the mid-grid ranks. The drivers did what they could. The Supertec engine, rebadged as Playlife, lacked power compared with the latest generation of power units. But the car was reliable enough and picked up points on a regular basis. But in 1999, the situation continued to deteriorate and the Benettons slipped down the order.

Despite these difficult conditions, the drivers did a good

job and their professionalism was never called into question. Fisichella even finished an unexpected second in Canada and even briefly led the race at the Nürburgring, before hitting a big puddle of water. At the end of the year, the team was sixth in the championship. The similarity with Tyrrell's history is amazing. Jackie Stewart's departure signalled the start of a decline, just as Michael Schumacher's did.

After the 2000 Australian Grand Prix, news emerged that Renault had bought the Benetton team for 120 million Euros. Flavio Briatore was brought back to supervise the transition period. The Benetton name remained until the end of the 2001 Japanese Grand Prix, having once got to the top of the F1 tree in record time. Luciano Benetton and his family had found a way to save face. Once again in 2000, it was Giancarlo Fisichella who salvaged something from the wreckage, allowing his team to finish a flattering fourth in the championship. His team-mate Alex Wurz, was often the victim of misfortune and would lose his drive for 2001.

Before the official return of Renault, 2001 would be a transitional year. Fisichella and Button would often pay the price. The new engine from the French company is packed with new ideas. During the first test session in Barcelona in Ferrari, the B 201 is slower than the previous year's car by six seconds. That would set the tone for the year. But despite the catastrophic results,

The post-Schumacher era was marked by a steady decline and a loss of identity.

Germany 1997: 11 years after their first win together, the Benetton team and Gerhard Berger enjoy their last win and the circle is completed.

Monaco 1996: Jean Alesi came very close to a superb win.

The team management changed hands three times, from Flavio Briatore to David Richards and then Rocco Benetton, before Briatore returned.

Benetton's presentations: 2000 in Barcelona, 2001 in Venice.

Canada 1998

Great Britain 1999

Giancarlo Fisichella, Flavio Briatore and Alexander Wurz.

the Benetton and Renault directors were confident about the future. As things turned out, the last few races did show signs of promise. Fisichella even managed a third place in the Belgian Grand Prix and gave the whole team a big shot in the arm.

Luciano Benetton, as colourful a character as his products, could have expected a dream send off. For his last year in Formula 1, he might have demanded that his cars shine and hit the front for one last time. But the hesitant progress of this new engine meant that was not in the realms of the possible. The Benettons spent months at the back of the grid. This difficult birth would allow Renault to reap the benefits of this daring investment. Wisely and with real class and realism, the man from Treviso accepted this one final challenge. He was able to walk away, his head held high. In this environment, where money and results are what matter, there is not much room for sentiment.

Formula 1 brought Benetton the clothing company a great deal. It gained world wide exposure through its exploits and success. It created a young, dynamic,

relaxed attitude. But it also brought much to the top level of motorsport. It came in with a new broom and swept away many of the old preconceived notions. Its communication skills opened up the sport to wider audience. In the middle of the Nineties, hot on the heels of the incredible Schumacher, Formula 1 was thrown into the spotlight and was the number one attraction. The departure of the German prodigy to pastures new,

broke the back of this young team. With his style, his ideas, his comments and his sense of humour, Flavio Briatore brought a lot to the world of Grands Prix. It is no coincidence that Renault plans to hang on to this man of the modern era.

And so, with very little fuss, with no fanfares or farewells, the Benetton cars completed their last lap at Suzuka on 14th October 2001. It was the end of a great story. ■

# F1 GIRLS

*Charmed*

*Charmed*

2

# THE 2002 GRANDS PRIX

*The 17 Dates on the 2002 Calendar*

Australia
Malaysia
Brasil
San Marino
Spain
Austria
Monaco
Canada
Europa
Great Britain
France
Germany
Hungary
Belgium
Italia
USA
Japan

Address:
Australian Grand Prix Corporation
220, Albert Road, P.O. Box 577,
South Melbourne, Victoria 3205
Australia
Tel: +61 3 92 58 71 00
Fax: +61 3 92 82 04 10
Internet: www.grandprix.com.au

Location: The circuit is to the south
of Melbourne, under ten kilometres
from the city centre.
Melbourne-Tullamarine
International Airport is 20
kilometres to the north of the city.

*Sunday 3rd March 2002*

# 01 AUSTRALIA
*Melbourne*

Start: 14h00 local time.
Distance: 58 laps of the 5.303 km circuit, total distance 307.574 km.
Attendance in 2001: 127,000 spectators on raceday.

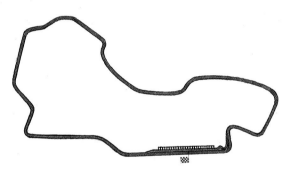

## The records to beat:
### Qualifying
M. Schumacher (Ferrari) in 2001: 1'26" 892 (219.707 km/h).
### Average race speed
D. Coulthard (McLaren) in 1997: 1h30'718 (203.926 km/h).
### Lap record
M. Schumacher (Ferrari) in 2001: 1'28" 214 (216.414 km/h).

## 2001 statistics:
### Pole position
M. Schumacher (Ferrari): 1'26" 892 (219.707 km/h).
### GP Results

| | | |
|---|---|---|
| 1. M. Schumacher (Ferrari) | 1h38'26"533 (187.464 km/h) | |
| 2. Coulthard (McLaren-Mercedes) | + 1"717 | |
| 3. Barrichello (Ferrari) | + 33"491 | |
| 4. Heidfeld (Sauber-Petronas) | + 1'11"479 | |
| 5. Frentzen (Jordan-Honda) | + 1'12"807 | |
| 6. Räikkönen (Sauber-Petronas) | + 1'24"143 | |

Since 1996, the Formula 1 season has kicked off on the other side of the world with a flight time in excess of twenty hours required to reach Melbourne. The local "Greens" made strenuous efforts to disrupt the first few runnings of the event, held in a suburban park. Albert Park is not without its charms, with its bucolic setting and eucalyptus trees, with the circuit snaking its way around a lake. Dozens of small sailing boats vie for space and mooring spots with the magnificent black and white swans, who have to put up with an increased noise level for the weekend.

Australians are keen on Formula 1 and this event is the highpoint of their year. They come in their thousands and show plenty of enthusiasm. They also hope that one day, they can cheer on home-grown talent like Mark Webber, the local hero who is knocking on the door of the sport. All the grandstands are named after world champions from the past. Australians have a blunt way of getting a message across and the crowds are given clear instructions about their expected behaviour. "If you drink then drive, you're a bloody idiot!" warn hosts of hoardings around the circuit. The Grand Prix is one big party and beer features heavily in the festivities. A fancy dress contest is staged every race day, with more and more spectators joining in the fun, showing plenty of imagination as they dress up as F1 drivers.

The ocean is just a stone's throw away and the local area is just like any seaside resort anywhere in the world, with the pavements littered with welcoming restaurants and bars, offering all sorts of delicacies.

The Australian GP is a big hit with the F1 folk, as it is very well organised and spending a week in the sunny Antipodes is a great way to start the season.

**Previous winners:**
2001: M. Schumacher (Ferrari)
2000: M. Schumacher (Ferrari)
1999: E. Irvine (Ferrari)
1998: M. Häkkinen (McLaren)
1997: D. Coulthard (McLaren)
1996: D. Hill (Williams)
1995: D. Hill (Williams)
1994: N. Mansell (Williams)
1993: A. Senna (McLaren)
1992: R. Patrese (Williams)
1991: A. Senna (McLaren)
1990: N. Piquet (Benetton)

Alain Prost (1985 and 86), Ayrton Senna (1991 and 93), Damon Hill (1995 and 96) and Michael Schumacher (2000 and 2001) all won the Australian Grand Prix twice.

The first winner was Keke Rosberg (Williams) in 1985 in Adelaide.

There have been 16 Australian Grands Prix: Adelaide from 1985 to 1995, Melbourne since 1996.

Address:
Sepang International Circuit
Jalan Pekeliling
64 000 Klia, Selangor, Malaysia
Tel: +603 85 26 20 00
Fax: +603 85 26 10 00
Internet: www.malaysiangp.com.my

Location: The Sepang circuit is in the south of the Malaysian Peninsula, 60 kilometres to the south of the capital city, Kuala Lumpur. The international airport is a mere 5 kilometres from the ultra-modern circuit.

*Sunday 17th March 2002*

Australia
**Malaysia**
Brasil
San Marino
Spain
Austria
Monaco
Canada
Europe
Grand Britain
France
Germany
Hungary
Belgique
Italy
USA
Japan

# MALAYSIA02
*Kuala Lumpur*

## Previous winners:
2001: M. Schumacher (Ferrari)
2000: M. Schumacher (Ferrari)
1999: E. Irvine (Ferrari)

The 2002 event will be the fourth Malaysian Grand Prix, which has always been held at the Sepang circuit, just outside Kuala Lumpur.

In 2001, the Malaysian Grand Prix was staged just five months after the first running of the event in October 2000. It had been a success and tens of thousands of spectators had come from all over the world. However, last year, despite a huge local promotion campaign in the streets of Kuala Lumpur, the grandstands were far from full. According to the local newspapers, the prices were too high for the average Malaysian, who does not have much disposable income.

The high-tech facility is the reference point by which all other F1 hosting circuits are judged. The futuristic look of the grandstands and infrastructure is really impressive.

Orchestrated with skill by Philippe Gurdjian, who also runs and promotes the Barcelona track as well as the new facility at Paul Ricard, the Malaysian Grand Prix is an example of how it should be done.

The locals are most likely to be out in force this year to see home-grown hero Alex Yoong, driving a Minardi with backing from several Malaysian sponsors. Just as last year, during the monsoon season, short but very violent storms can be expected during qualifying and the race.

## The records to beat:
### Qualifying
M. Schumacher (Ferrari) in 2001
1'13"780 (210.252 km/h).
### Average race speed
M. Schumacher (Ferrari) in 2000
1h35'54"256 (194.199 km/h).
### Lap record
M. Schumacher (Ferrari) in 2000
1'14"755 (207.509 km/h).

Start: 15h00 local time.
Distance: 56 laps of the 5.543 km circuit, total distance 310.408 km.
Attendance in 2001: 60,000 spectators on raceday.

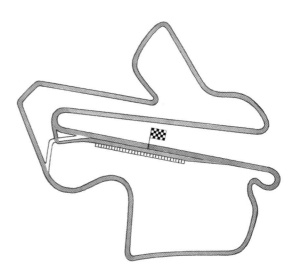

## 2001 statistics:
### Pole position
M. Schumacher (Ferrari): 1'13"780 (210.252 km/h).
### GP Results

| | | |
|---|---|---|
| 1. M. Schumacher (Ferrari) | 1h47'34"801 (170.030 km/h). | |
| 2. Barrichello (Ferrari) | + 23"660 | |
| 3. Coulthard (McLaren-Mercedes) | + 28"555 | |
| 4. Frentzen (Jordan-Honda) | + 46"543 | |
| 5. R. Schumacher (Williams-BMW) | + 48"233 | |
| 6. Häkkinen (McLaren-Mercedes) | + 48"606 | |

Australia
Malaysia
Brazil
San Marino
Spain
Austria
Monaco
Canada
Europe
Grande-Bretagne
France
Allemagne
Hongrie
Belgique
Italie
USA
Japon

Address:
Autodromo Jose Carlos Pace
Avenida Senador Teotonio Vilelia
259 - Sào Paolo, Brazil
Tel: +55 11 38 13 57 75
Fax: +55 11 38 12 40 79
Internet: www.gpbrasil.org

Location: Interlagos is about fifty kilometres to the south of Sao Paolo city centre. The airport of Sao Paolo-Guarulhos is on the other side of town, about fifty kilometres to the north.

# 03 BRAZIL

*Interlagos*

## Sunday 31st March 2002

Start: 14h00 local time.

Distance: 71 laps of the 4.309 km circuit, total distance 305.909 km.

Attendance in 2001: 80,000 spectators on raceday.

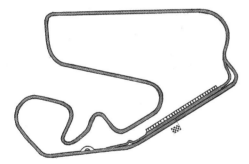

### The records to beat:

**Qualifying**

M. Schumacher (Ferrari) in 2001: 1'13"780 (210.252 km/h).

**Average race speed**

M. Schumacher (Ferrari) in 2000: 1h31'35"271 (200.403 km/h).

**Lap record**

M. Schumacher (Ferrari) in 2000: 1'14"755 (207.509 km/h).

### 2001 statistics:

**Pole position**

M. Schumacher (Ferrari): 1'13"780 (210.252 km/h).

**GP Results**

1. Coulthard (McLaren-Mercedes)  1h39'00"834
                                  (185.373 km/h)
2. M. Schumacher (Ferrari)          + 16"164
3. Heidfeld (Sauber-Petronas)       + 1 lap
4. Panis (BAR-Honda)                + 1 lap
5. Trulli (Jordan-Honda)            + 1 lap
6. Fisichella (Benetton-Renault)    + 1 lap

Every year, the prophets of doom love to predict the end of the Brazilian event at Interlagos. After the difficult years, which followed the death of Ayrton Senna, no one held out much hope for the future of this Grand Prix. But then, the arrival in the Ferrari camp of Rubens Barrichello, born just a stone's throw from the track, revived the event with huge crowds turning out. However, the paradox is amazing as the circuit which hosts the millionaire teams is surrounded by favellas, those awful, overpopulated slums. The very bumpy track is unique in being run anti-clockwise and is very demanding on both men and machinery.

One of the most beautiful tracks on the calendar. Torrential rain can change the outcome in a matter of a few moments. With high ambient temperatures, the track dries very quickly, giving a further twist to the drama for those who survive the downpour. There is a bronze bust of the Brazilian driver Carlos Pace at the entrance to the track. He won the 1975 Brazilian Grand prix. Nicknamed "Moco," he was very popular in Sao Paulo, but died tragically in a plane accident in 1977 and the circuit was then named in his memory. Situated in a suburb of this huge megalopolis, this is not the most popular weekend for the F1 folk. For many, the word Brazil evokes images of the tropics, the sun, fine sandy beaches and palm trees. However, Sao Paulo is more a case of pollution, insecurity and poverty for a large part of the population, who endure the strain common to living in one of the most densely populated cities in the world.

### Previous winners:

2001: D. Coulthard (McLaren)

2000: M. Schumacher (Ferrari)

1999: M. Häkkinen (McLaren)

1998: M. Häkkinen (McLaren)

1997: J. Villeneuve (Williams)

1996: D. Hill (Williams)

1995: M. Schumacher (Benetton)

1994: M. Schumacher (Benetton)

1993: A. Senna (McLaren)

1992: N. Mansell (Williams)

1991: A. Senna (McLaren)

1990: A. Prost (Ferrari)

Alain Prost won the Brazilian Grand Prix six times (1982, 84, 85, 87, 88 and 90).

Emerson Fittipaldi won the first Brazilian GP in 1973 at Interlagos. The 30th Brazilian Grand Prix will be held in 2002.

It was held at the Sao Paulo track of Interlagos from 1973 to 1978, then again in 1980 and every year since 1990 (20 times including 2002.)

It has also been run at Jacarepagua (Rio de Janeiro) in 1978 and from 1981 to 1989 (10 times.)

Australia
Malaysia
Brazil
San Marino
Spain
Austria
Monaco
Canada
Europe
Great-Britain
France
Germany
Hungary
Belgium
Italy
U.S.A.
Japan

**Address:**
Autodromo Internazionale Enzo e
Dino Ferrari
Sagis Spa, Via Fratelli Rosselli 2,
40 026 Imola, Italy.
Tel: +39 0 542 31 444
Fax: +39 0 542 30 420
Internet: www.autodromoimola.com

**Location:** The "Dino et Enzo
Ferrari" circuit is 35 kilometres
south-east of Bologna, just a few
hundred metres from the centre of
the small town of Imola.
The nearest airports are at Bologne
and Forli.

*Sunday
14th
April
2002*

# SAN MARINO 04
*Imola*

## Previous winners:
2001: R. Schumacher (Williams)
2000: M. Schumacher (Ferrari)
1999: M. Schumacher (Ferrari)
1998: D. Coulthard (McLaren)
1997: H.H. Frentzen (Williams)
1996: D. Hill (Williams)
1995: D. Hill (Williams)
1994: M. Schumacher (Benetton)
1993: A. Prost (Williams)
1992: N. Mansell (Williams)
1991: A. Senna (McLaren)
1990: R. Patrese (Williams)

Ayrton Senna (1988, 89 and 91)
and Alain Prost (1984, 86 and 93)
both won three times at Imola.

The first San Marino Grand Prix
was won by Nelson Piquet
(Brabham) on the 3rd May 1981 at
Imola.

There have been 22 San Marino
Grands Prix.

In 80 BC, in the glory days of the Roman empire, Imola was
known as Cornelli Forum and it was famous for its huge
amphitheatre where chariot races were staged.

We had to wait around two thousand years before
mechanical horses ruled the roost in Imola, after the race
track was built in 1950. Today, the circuit is called "Enzo e
Dino Ferrari" in honour of the local team, which always
draws the tifosi in their thousands. 1952 saw the debut of a
car bearing the then new Ferrari name, when a 340 sportscar
tested at the Imola track. It was the start of a long and
wonderful love story.

These days, if the cars carrying the black Prancing Horse
emblem retire before the end of the race, a large number of
spectators simply up sticks and leave the circuit.

The Emilia Romagna region is very welcoming, with just the
occasional traffic jam to deter the fans, who are not noted for
their patience. One has to be a stoic to make it to the nearby
motorways after the Grand Prix.

Traditionally, the San Marino Grand Prix marks the start of
the European season. It's the time to reacquaint oneself with
the delights of a full-on paddock. Every year, the
psychological war between the teams is fought out behind
the pits as the crews try and out-do one another with ever
more lavish motorhomes, designed to humble the
opposition.

## The records to beat:
### Qualifying
D. Coulthard (McLaren) in 2001: 1'23"054 (213.822 km/h).
### Average race speed
D. Coulthard (McLaren) in 1997: 1h30'28"718 (203.926 km/h).
### Lap record
R. Schumacher (Williams) in 2001: 1'25"524 (207.646 km/h).

Start: 14h00 local time.
Distance: 62 laps of the 4.933 km circuit, total distance 305.909 km.
Attendance in 2001: 120,000 spectators on raceday.

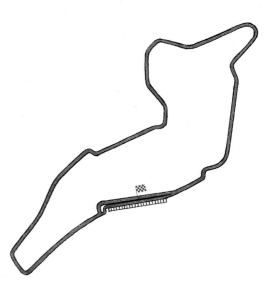

## 2001 statistics:
### Pole position
D. Coulthard (McLaren) in 2001: 1'23"054 (213.822 km/h).
### GP Results
1. R. Schumacher (Williams-BMW) 1h30'44"817
   (202.062 km/h)
2. Coulthard (McLaren-Mercedes)      + 4"352
3. Barrichello (Ferrari)      + 34"766
4. Häkkinen (McLaren-Mercedes)      + 36"315
5. Trulli (Jordan-Honda)      + 1'25"558
6. Frentzen (Jordan-Honda)      + 1 lap

Australia
Malaysia
Brazil
San Marino
*Spain*
Austria
Monaco
Canada
Europe
Great-Britain
France
Germany
Hungary
Belgium
Italy
USA
Japan

# 05 SPAIN
## *Barcelona*

Address:
Circuit de Catalunya
RACC, AP de Correus 27, 08160
Montmelo, Spain
Tel: +34 93 57 19 700
Fax: +34 93 57 22 772
Internet: www.circuitcat.com

Location: The circuit is about 20 kilometres north-east of Barcelona. The nearest airports are Barcelona to the south and Gerone to the north. The motorway linking Barcelona to France is just a kilometre away from the circuit.

*Sunday 25th April 2002*

Start: 14h00 local time.
Distance: 65 laps of the 4.730 km circuit, total distance 307.323 km.
Attendance in 2001: 100,000 spectators on raceday.

## The records to beat:
### Qualifying
J. Villeneuve (Williams) in 1997: 1'16"525 (222.421 km/h).
### Average race speed
J. Villeneuve (Williams) in 1997: 1h30'35"896 (200.314 km/h).
### Lap record
M. Schumacher (Ferrari) in 2001: 1'21"151 (209.831 km/h).

## 2001 statistics:
### Pole position
M. Schumacher (Ferrari): 1'18"201 (217.746 km/h).
### GP Results

| | | |
|---|---|---|
| 1. M. Schumacher (Ferrari) | 1h31'03"305 | |
| | (202.507 km/h) | |
| 2. Montoya (Williams-BMW) | + 40"738 | |
| 3. Villeneuve (BAR-Honda) | + 49"626 | |
| 4. Trulli (Jordan-Honda) | + 51"253 | |
| 5. Coulthard (McLaren-Mercedes) | + 51"616 | |
| 6. Heidfeld (Sauber-Petronas) | + 1'01"893 | |

Last year, Bernie Ecclestone had tasked one of his colleagues, Philippe Gurdjian, to take over the promotion of the Spanish Grand Prix. The mission proved successful. Situated around one hundred kilometres to the south of the Pyrenees, a large contingent of French race fans descended on the Catalan grandstands. New investment saw the pits enlarged as well as the money-spinning Paddock Club area. The Spanish Grand Prix has been held at Barcelona since 1991. Spectators in the main grandstand get a good view of much of the circuit, with few tracks offering such a panoramic vista of the action. It has to be said that this industrial region is not one of the prettiest appointments on the calendar. Fernando Alonso is one of the stars of the future, but in his new role as test driver for the Renault team, he will not enjoy the privilege of racing in front of his home crowd. This means Pedro De La Rosa will be the only local boy in action. King Juan Carlos is a Formula 1 fan and for the past few years he has turned up at the circuit and taken a keen interest in the event. On Sunday, he usually goes down the pit lane, meeting all the drivers and team owners, after the morning parade.

Barcelona hosts several winter testing sessions, as the technical challenge of the track is ideal for gathering data and working on set-up. Furthermore, the weather is usually favourable for this work. The drivers are therefore regular visitors to Catalunya and like the challenge of this track, as much as the spectators enjoy watching them in action. A good motorway network means that traffic is not a problem and the traffic jam nightmare, so common at other circuits, need not trouble the visitor here.

## Previous winners:
2001: M. Schumacher (Ferrari)
2000: M. Häkkinen (McLaren)
1999: M. Häkkinen (McLaren)
1998: M. Häkkinen (McLaren)
1997: J. Villeneuve (Williams)
1996: M. Schumacher (Ferrari)
1995: M. Schumacher (Benetton)
1994: D. Hill (Williams)
1993: A. Prost (Williams)
1992: N. Mansell (Williams)
1991: N. Mansell (Williams)
1990: A. Prost (Ferrari)

Alain Prost (1988, 90 and 93), Jackie Stewart (1969, 70 and 73) and Michael Schumacher (1995, 1996 and 2001) all won three times.

Juan Manuel Fangio won the first Spanish Grand Prix at Pedrables on the 28th October 1951.

2002 will be the 32nd running of the Spanish Grand Prix, held twice at Pedrables (Barcelona) in 1951 and 1954, 9 times at Jarama (Madrid) in 1968, 70, 72, 74, from 76 to 79 and in 81, 4 times at Montjuich (Barcelona) in 1969, 71, 73 and 75, 12 times at the Circuit of Catalunya (Barcelona) from 1991 to 2002.

Address:
A1-Ring Austria, Ring Management
Rennstrecken Betriegs Gmbh
8724 Spielberg, Austria.
Tel: +43 35 77 75 30
Fax: +43 35 77 75 3107
Internet: www.a1ring.at

Location: Located in the heart of the countryside, the A1 Ring used to be known as the Österreichring. It is a good 200 kilometres from the major Austrian cities, being 200 kilometres to the south east of Vienna and a hundred to the north of Graz. >>

Sunday
12th
May
2002

# AUSTRIA 06
*Spielberg*

>>
The motorway is less than a kilometre from the entrance to the track. Watch out for the Austrian police who take a dim view of speeding. Traffic jams around Vienna are also a problem on Sunday night.

## Previous winners:
2001: D. Coulthard (McLaren)
2000: M. Häkkinen (McLaren)
1999: E. Irvine (Ferrari)
1998: M. Häkkinen (McLaren)
1997: J. Villeneuve (Williams)
1987: N. Mansell (Williams)
1986: A. Prost (McLaren)
1985: A. Prost (McLaren)
1984: N. Lauda (McLaren)
1983: A. Prost (Renault)
1982: E. De Angelis (Lotus)
1981: J. Laffite (Ligier)
1980: J.P. Jabouille (Renault)

Alain Prost won three Austrian Grands Prix (1983, 85 and 86). The first Austrian GP was won by Lorenzo Bandini on the 23rd August 1964 in a Ferrari.
The 2002 event will be the 25th running of the Austrian Grand Prix, which has always been staged at Zeltweg.
In 1964, it was run at the airport. It was known as the Österreichring from 1970 to 1987.
Since 1997, the circuit has gone by the name of A1-Ring.

This year, the Austrian Grand Prix celebrates its 25th birthday. It has always been staged at the same venue. Lorenzo Bandini won the first event at the Zeltweg military airfield, on 23rd August 1964, at the wheel of a Ferrari. Within a few years, a fast and very demanding track was built to host the Formula 1 teams, snaking through the pine forests. In 1987, there was an accident at the start, then another at the restart, which saw several cars pile into one another. The track was deemed too narrow and dangerous and the event was simply taken off the Grand Prix calendar. Ten years later, following extensive modernisation work, the Austrian event was reinstated. The new track, which has some vestiges of the previous circuit, now meets all the current draconian safety criteria imposed by Formula 1 these days. In the past, this race was always staged in mid-August, much to the delight of the crowd which traditionally treated the event as a camping holiday. However, last year, the race was moved to May, when the surrounding mountains were still capped with snow. The Spielberg setting is both beautiful and impressive. There are not many hotels in the area, with most people staying in guest houses or farms in traditional "zimmer." The Austrians lay on a friendly welcome and it is a great way to spend a few days enjoying the natural beauty of the area.

### The records to beat:
#### Qualifying
M. Schumacher (Ferrari) in 2001: 1'09"562 (223.880 km/h).
#### Average race speed
D. Coulthard (McLaren) in 2001: 1h 27'45" 927 (209.977 km/h).
#### Lap record
D. Coulthard (McLaren) in 2001: 1'10"843 (219.832 km/h).

Start: 14h00 local time.
Distance: 71 laps of the 4.326 km circuit, total distance 307.146 km.
Attendance in 2001: 76,000 spectators on raceday.

### 2001 statistics:
#### Pole position
M. Schumacher (Ferrari): 1'09"562 (223.880 km/h).
#### GP Results
1. Coulthard (McLaren-Mercedes)   1h27'45"927
                                  (209.977 km/h)
2. M. Schumacher (Ferrari)        + 2"191
3. Barrichello (Ferrari)          + 2"528
4. Räikkönen (Sauber-Petronas)    + 41"594
5. Panis (BAR-Honda)              + 53"776
6. Verstappen (Arrows-Asiatech)   + 1 lap

Address:
Automobile Club de Monaco
23, Bd Albert-1er, BP 464, 98 012
Monaco Cedex
Tel: +377 93 15 26 00
Fax: +377 93 25 80 08
Internet: www.acm.mc

Location: The circuit is 18 kilometres to the east of Nice and is run on the streets of the Principality of Monaco. Of course, the nearest airport is Nice. From there, one can travel to Monaco by train, boat, car or helicopter.

*Sunday 26th May 2002*

# 07 MONACO
## *Monte-Carlo*

Start: 14h00 local time.
Distance: 78 laps of the 3.370 km circuit, total distance 262.860 km.
Attendance in 2001: 100,000 on raceday.

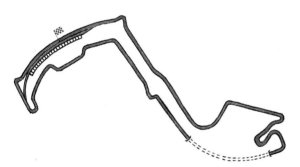

## The records to beat:
### Qualifying
D. Coulthard (McLaren) in 2001: 1'17"430 (156.683 km/h).
### Average race speed
M. Schumacher (Ferrari) in 2001: 1h47'22"561 (146.881km/h).
### Lap record
D. Coulthard (McLaren) in 2001: 1'19"424 (152.749 km/h).

## 2001 statistics:
### Pole position
D. Coulthard (McLaren): 1'17"430 (156.683 km/h).
### GP Results

| | | |
|---|---|---|
| 1. M. Schumacher (Ferrari) | 1h47'22"561 | |
| | (144.072 km/h) | |
| 2. Barrichello (Ferrari) | + 0"431 | |
| 3. Irvine (Jaguar) | + 30"698 | |
| 4. Villeneuve (BAR-Honda) | + 32"454 | |
| 5. Coulthard (McLaren-Mercedes) | + 1 lap | |
| 6. Alesi (Prost-Acer) | + 1 lap | |

For cynics and reactionaries alike, Monaco remains the Blue Riband event of the Formula 1 Grand Prix season. However, ticket prices are not within everyone's reach, so thousands of fans opt for a free view of this legendary event, perched on tree tops and hanging off the edge of the princely rock that overlooks the harbour. The grandstands are packed with a large contingent from across the border in Italy. Each square metre of the Principality is transformed to accommodate as many spectators as possible into the grandstands, although heavy demand always exceeds supply. Only a lucky 30,000 can get seats.

A project is currently underway to move the pits to the sea front, thus freeing up more space for grandstands. Luckily, there are other ways of watching the Monaco Grand Prix. If price is not an issue, then one can rent apartment balconies overlooking the track and this trend is growing. Many of the Monegasque residents rent out their homes and their terrasses for the weekend and this is particularly popular with corporate sponsors, who take over offices and flats in ever growing numbers.

In the space of just four days, the lucky owners earn enough money to pay their rent for a year. For those of a nautical disposition, boats and palatial yachts can be hired in the harbour, proving a great viewing spot for the race and for people-watching in the evening. It is the very apotheosis of the jet-set lifestyle.

But during the Monaco Grand Prix weekend, the core of the action is all on the track. Against the Mediterranean backdrop and with azure blue skies, the track from a bygone era never loses its fascination. Monaco is unique.

## Previous winners:
2001: M. Schumacher (Ferrari)
2000: D. Coulthard (McLaren)
1999: M. Schumacher (Ferrari)
1998: M. Häkkinen (McLaren)
1997: M. Schumacher (Ferrari)
1996: O. Panis (Ligier)
1995: M. Schumacher (Benetton)
1994: M. Schumacher (Benetton)
1993: A. Senna (McLaren)
1992: A. Senna (McLaren)
1991: A. Senna (McLaren)
1990: A. Senna (McLaren)

Ayrton Senna holds the record for most wins at Monaco with six (1987 and from 89 to 93).
Graham Hill (from 1963 to 65, and in 68 and 69) and Michael Schumacher (1994, 1995, 1997, 1999 and 2001) both won five times.
Alain Prost won four times (from 1984 to 1986 and in 88)

Juan Manuel Fangio won the first ever Monaco Grand Prix to count towards the world championship, on 21st May 1950 at the wheel of an Alfa Romeo.

This year's race will be the 53rd running of the event.

**Address:**
Grand Prix F1 du Canada Inc.
413 rue St Jacques, Suite 630
H2Y 1N9 Montréal, Canada.
Tel: +1 514 350 47 31
Fax: +1 514 350 00 07
Internet: www.grandprix.ca

**Location:** The Ile Notre Dame circuit is a few kilometres away from the city centre. The island was home to and International Expo and some events of the 1976 Olympic Games. Dorval International Airport is very close to >>

Sunday
9th
June
2002

# CANADA08
*Montréal*

>>
the centre of Montreal. The best way of getting from the town to the track is on the Metro.

## Previous winners:

2001: R. Schumacher (Williams)
2000: M. Schumacher (Ferrari)
1999: M. Häkkinen (McLaren)
1998: M. Schumacher (Ferrari)
1997: M. Schumacher (Ferrari)
1996: D. Hill (Williams)
1995: J. Alesi (Ferrari)
1994: M. Schumacher (Benetton)
1993: A. Prost (Williams)
1992: G. Berger (McLaren)
1991: N. Piquet (Benetton)
1990: A. Senna (McLaren)

Michael Schumacher has won four Canadian Grands Prix (1994, 97, 98 and 2000).
Nelson Piquet won three times here (1982, 84 and 91).
The first Canadian Grand Prix was won by Jack Brabham, on 27th August 1967, driving a Brabham-Repco at Mosport.
There have been 33 Canadian Grands Prix.
It has been held at:
Mosport, 8 times (1967, 69, from 1971 to 74 and in 76 and 77).
Mont-Tremblant, twice (1968 and 70).
Montréal, 24 times (from 1978 to 1986 and from 1988 to 2002).

Being so close to the vibrant city of Montreal, the event held on Ile Notre Dame is very popular with the Formula 1 fraternity. The Canadians are charming and welcoming and are very enthusiastic about their Grand Prix. The fact that Jacques Villeneuve is racing on a track named after his father certainly has something to do with it. Nevertheless, the spectators are keen on just about all the drivers.

Gilles Villeneuve won this Grand Prix in Montreal in 1978, the first time it was held there, at the wheel of a Ferrari. Back then, the North American races brought the curtain down on the season and were held in October. In '78, the temperature never rose much above freezing point.

The races in Montreal are often very exciting and incident packed. With a time difference which places the race on television in Europe towards the end of Sunday afternoon, means the Canadian GP draws a big international audience.

It might be just a few hours flying time from Europe, but it is a whole new world. Saint Catherine Street is the place to be over the weekend, all its restaurants decorated with some form of F1 publicity and packed out with locals and tourists alike. Indeed, the whole city throws itself into the spirit of the event with gusto.

## The records to beat:
### Qualifying
M. Schumacher (Ferrari) in 2001: 1'15"782 (210.018 km/h).
### Average race speed
R. Schumacher (Williams) in 2001: 1h34'31"522 (193.629 km/h).
### Lap record
R. Schumacher (Williams) in 2001: 1'17"205 (206.147 km/h).

Start: 13h00  local time.
Distance: 69 laps of the 4.421 km circuit, total distance 305.049 km.
Attendance in 2001: 110,000  spectators on the raceday.

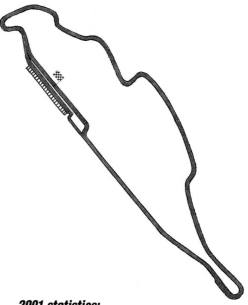

## 2001 statistics:
### Pole position
M. Schumacher (Ferrari): 1'15"782 (210.018 km/h).
### GP Results
1. R. Schumacher (Williams-BMW)  1h34'31"522
                                    (180.849 km/h)
2. M. Schumacher (Ferrari)          + 20"235
3. Häkkinen (McLaren-Mercedes)      + 40"672
4. Räikkönen (Sauber-Petronas)      + 1'08"115
5. Alesi (Prost-Acer)               + 1'10"435
6. De la Rosa (Jaguar)              + 1 lap

Address: Nürburgring Gmbh
53520 Nürburg, Germany
Tel: +49 (0)26 91 30 20
Fax: +49 (0)26 91 30 21 55
Internet: www.nürburgring.de

Location: The Nürburgring is 90 kilometres to the south east of Cologne and 60 kilometres north west of Koblenz. The main airports are at Cologne and Dusseldorf (120 km). The area is well served by an excellent motorway network, but getting to them on Sunday night can be fraught with traffic jams.

*Sunday 23rd June 2002*

# 09EUROPE

## *Nürburgring*

Start: 14h00 local time.

Distance: 59 laps of the 5.139 km circuit, total distance 303.201 km.

Attendance in 2001: 143,000 spectators on the Sunday.

Old track.
New map
to be confirmed.

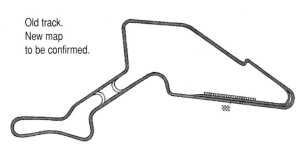

### The records (previous track):

**Qualifying**

M. Schumacher (Ferrari) in 2001: 1'14"960 (218.804 km/h).

**Average race speed**

M. Schumacher (Ferrari) in 2001: 1h29'42"724 (204.143 km/h).

**Lap record**

J.P. Montoya (Williams) in 2001: 1'18"354 (209.326 km/h).

### 2001 statistics:

**Pole position**

M. Schumacher (Ferrari): 1'14"960 (218.804 km/h).

**GP Results**

| | | |
|---|---|---|
| 1. M. Schumacher (Ferrari) | 1h29'42"724 | |
| | (204.143 km/h) | |
| 2. Montoya (Williams-BMW ) | + 4"217 | |
| 3. Coulthard (McLaren-Mercedes) | + 24"993 | |
| 4. R. Schumacher (Williams-BMW) | + 33"345 | |
| 5. Barrichello (Ferrari) | + 45"495 | |
| 6. Häkkinen (McLaren-Mercedes) | + 1'04"868 | |

Germany is currently Formula 1-mad. Michael Schumacher's undoubted supremacy, the excellent performances from his brother Ralf, as well as the high profile of car companies like Mercedes and BMW, have propelled this sport to the top of the popularity ladder. Hence the staging of two events in the country. The Nürburgring has a history of legendary proportions in motorsport.

Today, the old track is a tourist attraction which brings back memories of past glories. If you get the chance to drive round it, it is immediately apparent why it would be impossible to unleash 22 of today's Formula 1 cars around the old Nürburgring. Thus, the European Grand Prix is held on the new track, a mere stone's throw from the old. Watched over by the mysterious Nürburg castle, the circuit has borrowed some of the characteristics from Hockenheim, in that it has a huge stadium area, affording an excellent view of much of the action and is about to be lengthened by 583 metres. Just like the Spa circuit, its nearest neighbour, rain is a frequent visitor and the thermometer's higher reaches are seldom called into use. A chill wind is also on hand to cool the ardour of the most fiery fan. Despite this, the German crowd turns out in force. Around one hundred thousand fill the grandstands around the circuit.

This Grand Prix is not a big hit with the drivers and their teams. A bit of sunshine would be much appreciated.

### Previous winners:

2001: M. Schumacher (Ferrari)
2000: M. Schumacher (Ferrari)
1999: J. Herbert (Stewart)
1998: M. Häkkinen (McLaren)
1997: J. Villeneuve (Williams)
1996: J. Villeneuve (Williams)
1995: M. Schumacher (Benetton)
1994: M. Schumacher (Benetton)
1993: A. Senna (McLaren)
1985: N. Mansell (Williams)
1984: A. Prost (McLaren)

There have been 11 European Grands Prix.

Address: Silverstone Circuits Ltd
Northamptonshire, NN 12 8TN
Great Britain
Tel: +44 (0)1327 85 72 71
Fax: +44 (0)1327 85 76 63
Internet: www.silverstone-
circuit.co.uk

Location: Silverstone circuit is
about 110 km north-west of
London, 25 km south-east of
Northampton and 45 km from
Oxford. The nearest airports are
Birmingham (50 km), Luton and
London-Heathrow.

*Sunday*
*7th*
*July*
*2002*

# GREAT BRITAIN 10
*Silverstone*

## Previous winners:

2001: M. Häkkinen (McLaren)
2000: D. Coulthard (McLaren)
1999: D. Coulthard (McLaren)
1998: M. Schumacher (Ferrari)
1997: J. Villeneuve (Williams)
1996: J. Villeneuve (Williams)
1995: J. Herbert (Benetton)
1994: D. Hill (Williams)
1993: A. Prost (Williams)
1992: N. Mansell (Williams)
1991: N. Mansell (Williams)
1990: A. Prost (Ferrari)

Alain Prost (1983, 85, 89, 90 and
93) and Jim Clark (1962, 63, 64, 65
and 67) both won five times.
Nino Farina was the first winner of
a British Grand Prix on the 1st May
1950 at Silverstone, driving an Alfa
Romeo.
There have been 53 British Grands
Prix.
It has been held 35 times at
Silverstone (from 1950 to 58, in 60,
63, 65, 67, 69, 71, 73, 75, 77, 79,
81, 83, 85 and without interruption
since 1987.
Brands Hatch hosted the event
twelve times (in 1964, 66, 68, 70,
72, 74, 76, 80, 82, 84 and 86
alternating with Silverstone).
It was staged 5 times at Aintree (in
1955, 57,59 ,61 and 62).

A reader wrote in to an English magazine about his
Silverstone experiences. He reckoned he had spent
over 120 hours stuck in the legendary traffic jams
attending the British GP at the Northamptonshire
circuit since 1992. Under threat from FIA over this
problem, the organisers, Octagon Motorsport have
made various improvements and also restricted the
gate this year, while increasing ticket prices to ensure
the revenue does not suffer.
This means only 60,000 fans will get in on Sunday,
instead of the usual 90,000, who brave whatever the
weather throws at them to attend this historical event.
That means around a third of those who usually make
the trip will now have to settle down in front of their
televisions.
The circuit, which claims it is "the heart of motor sport"
is going through a bad patch at the moment. A three
day general admission ticket, allowing you to brave the
traffic and the queues will cost 310 Euros.
It makes this event the most expensive on the
calendar. Furthermore, you will need to pay a further
70 Euros for the privilege of parking, although you
might have to pay more to have the car towed out if it
pours with rain!
The fans are not happy; many of them voting with their
feet and giving up on Silverstone in favour of heading
off to races in Belgium, Germany or France, where
ticket prices are lower. Tradition is making way for
pragmatism, although when the sun shines, this track
still has a certain charm. The energetic efforts of the
B.R.D.C. (The British Racing Drivers Club) led by its
president, Sir Jackie Stewart has met with some
success in saving the British Grand Prix. But it was a
close call. Plans for a new circuit have been drawn up,
but the most pressing problem remains the traffic
situation. A new bypass is being built and should be
completed in time for the summer date, consigning the
Silverstone snail-paced approach to a thing of the
past.

Start: 13h00 local time.
Distance: 60 laps of the 5.141 km circuit, total distance 308,356 km
Attendance in 2001 : 90,000 spectators on raceday.

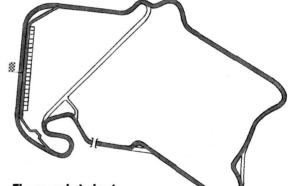

## The records to beat:
### Qualifying
M. Schumacher (Ferrari) in 2001: 1'20"447 (230.059 km/h).
### Average race speed
M. Häkkinen (McLaren) in 2001: 1h25'33"770 (216.231 km/h).
### Lap record
M. Häkkinen (McLaren) in 2001: 1'23"405 (221.900 km/h).

## 2001 statistics:
### Pole position
M. Schumacher (Ferrari): 1'20"447 (230.059 km/h).
### GP Results

1. Häkkinen (McLaren-Mercedes)  1h25'33"770
                                (216.231 km/h)
2. M. Schumacher (Ferrari)       + 33"646
3. Barrichello (Ferrari)         + 59"280
4. Montoya (Williams-BMW)        + 1'08"772
5. Räikkönen (Sauber-Petronas)   + 1 lap
6. Heidfeld (Sauber-Petronas)    + 1 lap

# 11 FRANCE
## Magny-Cours

Address:
Circuit de Nevers-Magny-Cours
Technopole, 58470 Magny-Cours
France.
Tel: +33 (0)3 86 21 80 00
Fax: +33 (0)3 86 21 80 80
Internet: www.magnyf1.com

Location: The Nevers-Magny-Cours circuit is 12 kilometres to the south of Nevers, 250 kilometres to the south of Paris and 220 kilometres to the north of Lyon. There are no international airports within a 200 kilometres radius, which makes it a nightmare for foreign visitors.

Sunday 21st July 2002

Start: 14h00 local time.
Distance: 72 laps of the 4,251 km circuit, total distance 305,886 km.
Attendance in 2001: 120,000 spectators on raceday.

In order to avoid a clash with the World Cup Soccer finals, where the French team hopes to play a prominent role, the Magny-Cours organisers arranged a date swap with Silverstone. Therefore the French Grand Prix will take place in the second half of July. Criticised for being in the middle of nowhere, the area which hosts the French round of the world championship does have some appealing features. However, the locals do charge extortionate prices to accommodate guests, making the most of the fact that hotels are few and far between. Consolation can be found in the excellent standard of the restaurants and by sampling the wonderful local wines.

The circuit infrastructure is up to the required standard. Every year, additional grandstands are erected as more and more spectators flock to the race from all over Europe, to ensure that the Nevers-Magny-Cours Grand Prix is always a success.

**Previous winners:**
2001: M. Schumacher (Ferrari)
2000: D. Coulthard (McLaren)
1999: H. H. Frentzen (Jordan)
1998: M. Schumacher (Ferrari)
1997: M. Schumacher (Ferrari)
1996: D. Hill (Williams)
1995: M. Schumacher (Benetton)
1994: M. Schumacher (Benetton)
1993: A. Prost (Williams)
1992: N. Mansell (Williams)
1991: N. Mansell (Williams)
1990: A. Prost (Ferrari)

Alain Prost won the French Grand Prix six times (1981, 83, from 88 to 90 and 93).
Michael Schumacher was the winner five times (1994, 95, 97, 98 and 2001).
Juan Manuel Fangio won the first Grand Prix of France at Reims on the 2nd July 1950, driving an Alfa Romeo.
There have been 51 French Grands Prix. Reims: (11 times) 1950, 51,53, 54, 56, from 58 to 61,63 and 66. Rouen: (5 times) 1952, 57, 62, 64 and 68. Clermont-Ferrand: (4 times) 1965, 69, 70 and 72. Le Mans: (once) 1967. Le Castellet: (14 times) 1971, 73, 75, 76, 78, 80, 82, 83, from 85 to 90. Dijon-Prenois: (5 times) 1974, 77, 79, 81 and 84. Magny-Cours: (10 times) from 1991 to 2001.

### 2001 statistics:
**Pole position**
R. Schumacher (Williams): 1'12"989 (209.669 km/h)
**GP Results**
1. M. Schumacher (Ferrari)  1h33'35"636
   (196.093 km/h)
2. R. Schumacher (Williams-BMW)  + 10"399
3. Barrichello (Ferrari)  + 16"381
4. Coulthard (McLaren-Mercedes)  + 17"106
5. Trulli (Jordan-Honda)  + 1'08"285
6. Heidfeld (Sauber-Petronas)  + 1 lap

### The records to beat:
**Qualifying**
R. Schumacher (Williams) in 2001
1'12"989 (209.669 km/h)
**Average race speed**
M. Schumacher (Ferrari) in 1998
1h33'35"636 (196.093 km/h)
**Lap record**
D. Coulthard (McLaren) in 2001
1'16"088 (201.130 km/h)

Address: Hockenheim Gmbh,
Postfach 1106, 68754 Hockenheim,
Germany
Tel: +49 62 05 40 31
Fax: +49 62 05 95 02 99
Internet: www.hockenheim.de

Location: The circuit is 90
kilometres to the south of Frankfurt,
110 kilometres to the north east of
Stuttgart and around twenty
kilometres from the old city of
Heidelberg. There are plenty of
motorways in the area, making
access a simple affair.

*Sunday
28th
July
2002*

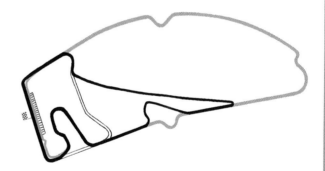

# GERMANY 12
*Hockenheim*

## Previous winners:

2001: R. Schumacher (Williams)
2000: R. Barrichello (Ferrari)
1999: E. Irvine (Ferrari)
1998: M. Häkkinen (McLaren)
1997: G. Berger (Benetton)
1996: D. Hill (Williams)
1995: M. Schumacher (Benetton)
1994: G. Berger (Ferrari)
1993: A. Prost (Williams)
1992: N. Mansell (Williams)
1991: N. Mansell (Williams)
1990: A. Senna (McLaren)

Juan Manuel Fangio (1954, 56 and
57), Nelson Piquet (1981, 86 and
87) and Ayrton Senna (1988, 89
and 90) all won the German Grand
Prix three times.
Alberto Ascari won the first German
Grand Prix on 29th July 1951 at the
Nürburgring driving an Alfa Romeo.
2002 will be the 50th running of the
German Grand Prix.
The German Grand Prix has been
held at:
- Nürburgring: (23 times) from 1951
to 54, from 56 to 58, from 61 to 69 ,
from 71 to 76 and in 1985. Now, it
is home to the European Grand
Prix since 1999.
- Avus near Berlin: (once) in 1959.
- Hockenheim: (26 times) in 1970,
from 1977 to 84 and since 1986.

This old oval circuit was re-opened for racing in 1966.
At the time, the track was made up of a twisty section
which ran through a giant amphitheatre, known as the
Stadium. This was linked to two very long straights
through the forest. Following the death of Jim Clark in
a Formula 2 race in 1968, chicanes were introduced to
bring down the speeds on these high speed sections.
A major overhaul began this January and will be
finished in time for the Grand Prix. The run through the
forest was never very interesting and it has quite
simply been removed. Now, a new section will link the
first and third chicanes. This new section will provide
room for additional grandstands, which means that the
Hockenheimring will now be able to accommodate up
to 120,000 spectators.
Supporters of the brothers Schumacher will now be
even more numerous. This is one of the most colourful
events on the calendar and seeing the cars through
the stadium section is particularly impressive. Every
time Michael Schumacher's red Ferrari breaks into
view, it is greeted with multi-coloured fire crackers,
waving flags and a deafening roar from the crowd. The
noise also serves to wake up those spectators who
might be dozing off after a particularly hard night in the
camp sites. Beer runs like water and the fans keep a
tally of their drinking by building impressive pyramids
of cans and bottles outside their tents.

Start: 14h00 local time.
Distance: 67 laps of the 4. 489 km circuit, total distance 300.763 km.
Attendance in 2001: 120,000 spectators on raceday.

## The records (previous track)
### Qualifying
J.P. Montoya (Williams) in 2001: 1'38"117 (250.415 km/h).
### Average race speed
R. Schumacher (Williams) in 2001: 1h18'17"873 (235.351 km/h).
### Lap record
J.P. Montoya (Williams) in 2001: 1'41"808 (241.336 km/h).

## 2001 statistics:
### Pole position
J.P. Montoya (Williams): 1'38"117 (250.415 km/h).
### GP Results
1. R. Schumacher (Williams-BMW)  1h18'17"873
                               (235.351 km/h)
2. Barrichello (Ferrari)              + 46"117
3. Villeneuve (BAR-Honda)         + 1'02"806
4. Fisichella (Benetton-Renault)   + 1'03"477
5. Button (Benetton-Renault)       + 1'05"454
6. Alesi (Prost-Acer)                 + 1'05"950

Melbourne
Malaysia
Brazil
San Marino
Spain
Austria
Monaco
Magny-Cours
France
Germany
Germany
Hungary
Belgium
Italy
USA
Japan

Address: Hungaroring Sport Rt
2146 Mogyorod PF 10, Hungary
Tel: +36 28 44 44 44
Fax: +36 28 44 18 60
Internet: www.hungaroring.hu

Location: The Hungaroring is 20 kilometres to the north east of Budapest and its international airport at Ferihegy. A motorway links the city to the track and on Sunday night, the trick is to jump on the back of a police-escorted convoy, to avoid the inevitable traffic jams.

*Sunday 18th August 2002*

# 13 HUNGARY
*Budapest*

Start: 14h00 local time.

Distance: 77 laps of the 3,975 km circuit, total distance 306.075 km.

Attendance in 2001: 110,000 spectators on raceday.

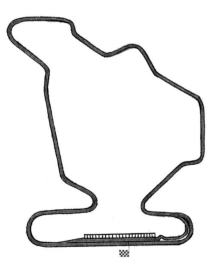

As communism crumbled, Hungary was the first Eastern Bloc country to stage a Formula 1 Grand Prix, back in 1986. Now, Russia, under the guidance of Tom Walkinshaw, is due to welcome the big circus in the suburbs of Moscow, possibly in 2003. Bernie Ecclestone himself has personally visited the site, before the work begins.

Traditionally held in mid-August, this year's event will be the 17th running of the Hungarian race.

The Germans, the Austrians and, surprisingly, the Finns, flock here in their thousands. The ticket price is not within reach of most of the locals. It is invariably hot and sunny and Budapest, one of the most beautiful cities in Europe, has plenty to offer the tourist, as it is rich in history. Up until last year, prostitution was rife around the track. A huge advertising panel near the entrance, proclaimed the delights on offer in the "Erotik Camping!" It was considered a boon for lonely campers! But last year, the authorities put a stop to it.

The track is very twisty and not a big favourite with the drivers. Overtaking, already rare in this sport, is virtually impossible in Budapest and so the race can often be processional. In the height of the summer holidays, lethargy and drowsiness can take its toll on even the most avid of television viewers.

### 2001 statistics:
#### Pole position
M. Schumacher (Ferrari): 1'14"059 (193.224 km/h).

#### GP Results
| | | |
|---|---|---|
| 1. M. Schumacher (Ferrari) | 1h41'49"675 | |
| | 180.348 km/h | |
| 2. Barrichello (Ferrari) | + 3"363 | |
| 3. Coulthard (McLaren-Mercedes) | + 3"940 | |
| 4. R. Schumacher (Williams-BMW) | + 49"687 | |
| 5. Häkkinen (McLaren-Mercedes) | + 1'10"293 | |
| 6. Heidfeld (Sauber-Petronas) | + 1 lap | |

### The records to beat:
#### Qualifying
M. Schumacher (Ferrari) in 2001: 1'14"059 (193.224 km/h).

#### Average race speed
M. Schumacher (Ferrari) in 2001: 1h41' 49"675 (180.348 km/h).

#### Lap record
M. Häkkinen (McLaren) in 2001: 1'16"723 (186.515 km/h).

### Previous winners:
2001: M. Schumacher (Ferrari)
2000: M. Häkkinen (McLaren)
1999: M. Häkkinen (McLaren)
1998: M. Schumacher (Ferrari)
1997: J. Villeneuve (Williams)
1996: J. Villeneuve (Williams)
1995: D. Hill (Williams)
1994: M. Schumacher (Benetton)
1993: D. Hill (Williams)
1992: A. Senna (McLaren)
1991: A. Senna (McLaren)
1990: T. Boutsen (Williams)

Ayrton Senna (1988, 1991 and 92) and Michael Schumacher (1994, 1998 and 2001) both won the Hungarian Grand Prix three times Jacques Villeneuve (1996 and 97) and Damon Hill (1993 and 95) both won twice in Budapest. Nelson Piquet was the first Hungarian Grand Prix winner, at the wheel of a Williams on 10th August 1986.

2002 will be the 17th running of the Hungarian Grand Prix, which has always been held at Budapest's Hungaroring.

Address:
Circuit de Spa-Francorchamps
55, route du circuit, 4790
Francorchamps, Belgium
Tel: +32 (0)87 27 51 46
Fax: +32 (0)87 27 55 51
Internet:
www.spa-francorchamps.be

Location: The Spa-Francorchamps circuit is in the east of Belgium, in the Walloon area of the country, halfway between Luxembourg and Brussels. It is 50 kilometres to the south east of Liege, 50 kilometres >>

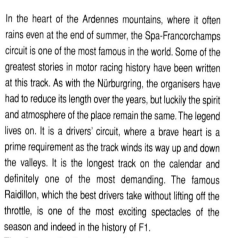

# BELGIUM 14
## Spa-Francorchamps

>> from Aix-la-Chapelle in Germany and a hundred from Brussels. A good motorway network makes it easy to get to Spa, but watch out for the Belgian police and their speed traps!

## Previous winners:

2001: M. Schumacher (Ferrari)
2000: M. Häkkinen (McLaren)
1999: D. Coulthard (McLaren)
1998: D. Hill (Jordan)
1997: M. Schumacher (Ferrari)
1996: M. Schumacher (Ferrari)
1995: M. Schumacher (Benetton)
1994: D. Hill (Williams)
1993: D. Hill (Williams)
1992: M. Schumacher (Benetton)
1991: A. Senna (McLaren)
1990: A. Senna (McLaren)

Ayrton Senna (1985, 88, 89, 90 and 91) and Michael Schumacher (1992, 95, 96, 97 and 2001) both won five times at Spa. Jim Clark won here four times (1962, 63, 64 and 65) There have been 48 Belgian Grands Prix.
It has been staged 36 times at Spa-Francorchamps, from 1950 to 1956, in 1958, from 1960 to 1968, in 1970 and 1983 and without interruption, since 1985. It was run twice at Nivelles (1972 and 1974). Finally, it was also held at Zolder ten times (1973, from 1975 to 1982 and in 1984).

In the heart of the Ardennes mountains, where it often rains even at the end of summer, the Spa-Francorchamps circuit is one of the most famous in the world. Some of the greatest stories in motor racing history have been written at this track. As with the Nürburgring, the organisers have had to reduce its length over the years, but luckily the spirit and atmosphere of the place remain the same. The legend lives on. It is a drivers' circuit, where a brave heart is a prime requirement as the track winds its way up and down the valleys. It is the longest track on the calendar and definitely one of the most demanding. The famous Raidillon, which the best drivers take without lifting off the throttle, is one of the most exciting spectacles of the season and indeed in the history of F1.

The German border is very close and fans arrive en masse in Spa, to cheer on Michael Schumacher, who is a specialist on this track, where he made his F1 debut in 1991. The changing weather conditions often play a key role in the final outcome.

Despite improvements to the approach roads, getting out on Sunday night is always a nightmare, with the stupid behaviour of the local traffic police to blame.

Nevertheless, the Grand Prix at Spa is definitely one of the classics of the season, just like Monaco or Monza. Make sure to bring your umbrella. The rain clouds love the area and always want to be part of the action.

## The records to beat:
### Qualifying
M. Häkkinen (McLaren) in 1998: 1'48"682 (230.809 km/h).
### Average race speed
M. Schumacher (Ferrari) in 2001: 1h08'05"002 (221.050 km/h).
### Lap record
M. Schumacher (Ferrari) in 2001: 1'49"758 (228.546 km/h).

Start: 14h00 local time.
Distance: 44 laps of the 6.968 km circuit, total distance 306.592 km.
Attendance in 2001: 85,000 spectators on raceday.

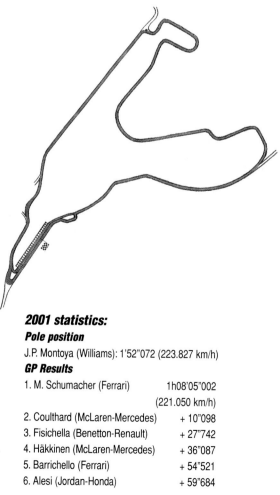

## 2001 statistics:
### Pole position
J.P. Montoya (Williams): 1'52"072 (223.827 km/h)
### GP Results

| | | |
|---|---|---|
| 1. M. Schumacher (Ferrari) | 1h08'05"002 | |
| | (221.050 km/h) | |
| 2. Coulthard (McLaren-Mercedes) | + 10"098 | |
| 3. Fisichella (Benetton-Renault) | + 27"742 | |
| 4. Häkkinen (McLaren-Mercedes) | + 36"087 | |
| 5. Barrichello (Ferrari) | + 54"521 | |
| 6. Alesi (Jordan-Honda) | + 59"684 | |

Address: Automobile Club di Milano-Corso Venezia 43
20121 Milano, Italy
Tel: +39 02 77 45 228
Fax: +39 02 78 18 44
Internet: www.monzanet.it

Location: The Monza circuit is located in the town park, about fifteen kilometres from Milan. It is well served by several motorways. Linate and Malpensa are the two international airports in the area. Watch out for the traditional traffic jams on Sunday night. Don't lose your cool!

*Sunday 15th September 2002*

Start: 14h00 local time.
Distance: 53 laps of the 5.793 km circuit, total distance 306.764 km.
Attendance in 2001: 95,000 spectators on raceday.

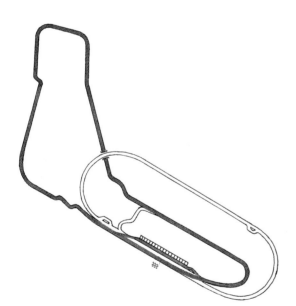

Along with Nürburgring, Spa, Silverstone and Monaco, Monza is one of the last links with Formula 1's glorious past. It is one of the key dates on the calendar. The Italian Grand Prix has always been staged at Monza, since the world championship started in 1950, with the exception of 1980 when the honour of holding this event fell to Imola. Year after year, the track was modified to keep up with safety requirements and traces of the banking still exists today. As the circuit is situated in the city park, the ecologists are making life difficult for the organisers of the event. Every time a tree is felled, it is considered a sacrilege. The grandstand area will be totally rebuilt for the 2002 edition of the Italian Grand Prix.

Monza fever is a unique phenomenon and it has to be experienced to be believed. In practice, every time a Ferrari takes to the track, it is considered an event of major importance. If, during qualifying, a red car takes pole position, the circuit commentator emulates the Brazilian soccer commentators when a goal was scored by Pele, during the 1970 World Cup. As summer draws to a close, the atmosphere in the park and the mood created by the tifosi is quite unbelievable. Last year, events in the United States threw a dark cloud over the temple of motor sport. On top of that, Juan Pablo Montoya had the nerve to beat the Ferraris.

### 2001 statistics:
**Pole position**
J.P. Montoya (Williams): 1'22"216 (253.658 km/h).

**GP Results**

| | | |
|---|---|---|
| 1. Montoya (Williams-BMW) | 1h16'58"493 | |
| | (239.103 km/h) | |
| 2. Barrichello (Ferrari) | + 5"175 | |
| 3. R. Schumacher (Williams-BMW) | + 17"335 | |
| 4. M. Schumacher (Ferrari) | + 24"993 | |
| 5. De la Rosa (Jaguar) | + 1'14"984 | |
| 6. Villeneuve (BAR-Honda) | + 1'22"469 | |

### The records to beat:
**Qualifying**
J.P. Montoya (Williams) in 2001: 1'22"216 (253.658 km/h).

**Average race speed**
J.P. Montoya (Williams) in 2001: 1h16'58"493 (239.103 km/h).

**Lap record**
R. Schumacher (Williams) in 2001: 1'25"073 (245.140 km/h).

**Previous winners:**
2001: J.P. Montoya (Williams)
2000: M. Schumacher (Ferrari)
1999: H.H. Frentzen (Jordan)
1998: M. Schumacher (Ferrari)
1997: D. Coulthard (McLaren)
1996: M. Schumacher (Ferrari)
1995: J. Herbert (Benetton)
1994: D. Hill (Williams)
1993: D. Hill (Williams)
1992: A. Senna (McLaren)
1991: N. Mansell (Williams)
1990: A. Senna (McLaren)

Nelson Piquet won this G.P. four times (1980, 83, 86 and 87). Juan Manuel Fangio (1953,54 and 55), Stirling Moss (1956, 57 and 59), Ronnie Peterson (1973, 74 and 76), Alain Prost (1981,85 and 89) and Michael Schumacher (1996, 98 and 2000) all won three times in Italy.
Giuseppe Farina won the first Italian Grand Prix to count towards the world championship, on 3rd September 1950 at Monza.

2002 will see the 53rd running of the Italian Grand Prix. It has always been held at Monza except in 1980 when it was run at Imola.

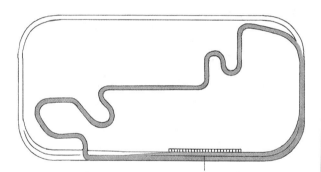

Address:
International Motor Speedway
4790 West 16th Street
Indianapolis, Indiana 46 222 USA
Tel: +1 317 484 67 80
Fax: +1 317 484 64 82
Internet: www.usgpindy.com

Location: Indianapolis is the capital of the State of Indiana. The famous oval circuit which provides the backdrop to the F1 circuit, is about ten kilometres from the city centre, in the western suburbs.

*Sunday 29th September 2002*

# UNITED-STATES16
*Indianapolis*

## Previous winner:

2001: M. Häkkinen (McLaren)
2000: M. Schumacher (Ferrari)
1991: A. Senna (McLaren)
1990: A. Senna (McLaren)
1989: A. Prost (Ferrari)
1988: A. Senna (McLaren)
1987: A. Senna (Lotus)
1986: A. Senna (Lotus)
1985: K. Rosberg (Williams)
1984: N. Piquet (Brabham)
1984: K. Rosberg (Williams)
1983: J. Watson (McLaren)
1983: M. Alboreto (Tyrrell))

This will be the 46th running of the United States Grand Prix.

Here are details of circuits used: Sebring once (1959), Riverside once (1960), Watkins Glen 20 times (from 1961 to 1980), Long Beach 8 times (from 1976 to 1983), Las Vegas 2 times (1981 and 1982), Detroit 7 times (from 1982 to 1988), Dallas once (1984), Phoenix 3 times (from 1989 to 1991) and Indianapolis from 2000

Ayrton Senna won five US Grands Prix (1986, 87, 89, 90 and 91), Bruce McLaren won the first US Grand Prix, held at Sebring on 12th December 1959. The US Grand Prix returned to the calendar in 2000, after a long absence.

After the acts of terrorism on September 11, Bernie Ecclestone and the organiser, Tony George, moved heaven and earth to keep the event on the calendar, despite the impending American military action in Afghanistan. There was much talk about whether this was the right or the wrong decision, but in the end it proved to be the right one. On race day, every spectator was handed a small Stars and Stripes flag, which they proudly waved throughout the race. The only sign of the international crisis could be seen in the hands of enterprising stall holders, selling T-shirts with the slogan: "Wanted dead or alive - Bin Laden."
The track itself is nothing special. Despite that, this event deserves its place on the F1 world championship calendar.
Against the backdrop of the famous and grandiose Indianapolis oval, the crowds, who have only got to grips with the stars of Formula 1 since 2000, give everyone a very warm reception.
The country eagerly awaits the day when American drivers compete in F1 and much hinges on a sponsorship programme undertaken by Red Bull, with this single aim in mind.

Start: 13h00 local time.
Distance: 73 laps of the 4.192 km circuit, total distance 306.016 km.
Attendance in 2001: 200,000 spectators on raceday.

## The records to beat:
### Qualifying
M. Schumacher (Ferrari) in 2001: 1'11"708 (210.453 km/h).
### Average race speed
M. Häkkinen (McLaren) in 2001: 1h32'42"840 (198.038 km/h).
### Lap record
J.P. Montoya (Williams) in 2001: 1'14"448 (202.708 km/h).

## 2001 statistics:
### Pole position
M. Schumacher (Ferrari): 1'11"708 (210,453 km/h.
### GP Results
| | | |
|---|---|---|
| 1. Häkkinen (McLaren-Mercedes) | 1h32'42"84 | |
| | (198.038 km/h) | |
| 2. M. Schumacher (Ferrari) | + 11"046 | |
| 3. Coulthard (McLaren-Mercedes) | + 12"043 | |
| 4. Trulli (Jordan-Honda) | + 57"423 | |
| 5. Irvine (Jaguar) | + 1'12"434 | |
| 6. Heidfeld (Sauber-Petronas) | + 1'12"996 | |

Address:
Suzuka Circuitland Co Ltd
7992 Ino-cho, Suzuka-shi, Mie-kem
510-0295, Japan
Tel: +81 593 78 36 20
Fax: +81 593 78 36 25
Internet: www.suzukacircuit.co.jp

Location: The Suzuka circuit is 500 kilometres to the south east of Tokyo, 150 kilometres to the east of Osaka and 70 kilometres from Nagoya. Japan really is a different world. The circuit hotel is reserved for drivers and team bosses. >>

# 17 JAPAN

*Suzuka*

**Sunday 13th October 2002**

Start: 14h30 local time.
Distance: 53 laps of the 5.846 km circuit, total distance 310.596 km
Attendance in 2001: 150,000 spectators on raceday.

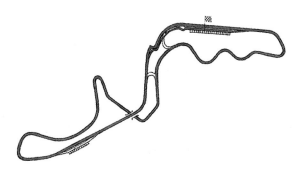

## The records to beat:
### Qualifying
M. Schumacher (Ferrari) in 2001: 1'32"484 (228.260 km/h).
### Average race speed
M. Schumacher (Ferrari) in 2001: 1h 27'33" 298 (212.664 km/h).
### Lap record
R. Schumacher (Williams) in 2001: 1'36"944 (217.573 km/h).

## 2001 statistics:
### Pole position
M. Schumacher (Ferrari): 1'32"484 (228.260 km/h).
### GP Results
| | | |
|---|---|---|
| 1. M. Schumacher (Ferrari) | 1h27'33"298 | |
| | (212.664 km/h) | |
| 2. Montoya (Williams-BMW) | + 3"154 | |
| 3. Coulthard (McLaren-Mercedes) | + 23"262 | |
| 4. Häkkinen (McLaren-Mercedes) | + 35"539 | |
| 5. Barrichello (Ferrari) | + 36"544 | |
| 6. R. Schumacher (Williams-BMW) | + 37"122 | |

Formula 1 is sure to stage a comeback in the land of the rising sun. After the death of Ayrton Senna, Honda's withdrawal from the sport and the absence of any decent Japanese drivers, the sport's popularity took a dive. Takuma Sato's arrival in the Jordan camp and Toyota joining the fray will revitalise interest for the Nippon people in this grand prix. Rivalry between Honda and Toyota will no doubt polarise the supporters into different camps.

Suzuka circuit is situated in an amusement park built for the workers and families from the surrounding Honda factories and this year it should be as packed as in the past. It has been years since spectators have camped out on the pavement on Saturday night, waiting outside the gates to the circuit to be the first through the doors on the day of the grand prix.

This country is definitely the hardest to get used to for the F1 folk. Hotel rooms are tiny and the food is an acquired taste and pretty strange. However, those pining for a taste of Europe can stop off in a bakery run by a Frenchman at the circuit hotel, but it does not come cheap.

The Japanese Grand Prix is an enjoyable event, although for some, the best thing about it is that is the final round of the season and the start of the holidays.

>> The mechanics and other team personnel and the press all stay in small hotels in towns around the track and first timers feel really out of place.

## Previous winners:
2001: M. Schumacher (Ferrari)
2000: M. Schumacher (Ferrari)
1999: M. Häkkinen (McLaren)
1998: M. Häkkinen (McLaren)
1997: M. Schumacher (Ferrari)
1996: D. Hill (Williams)
1995: M. Schumacher (Ferrari)
1994: D. Hill (Williams)
1993: A. Senna (McLaren)
1992: N. Mansell (Williams)
1991: G. Berger (McLaren)
1990: N. Piquet (Benetton)

M. Schumacher has won four Japanese Grands Prix (1995, 1997, 2000 and 2001). M. Häkkinen (1998 and 99), D. Hill (1994 and 96) and G. Berger (1987 and 91) all won twice. Mario Andretti was the first winner of a Japanese Grand Prix at the Mount Fuji circuit on 24th October 1976 at the wheel of a Lotus. 2002 will see the 18th running of the Japanese Grand Prix. Mount Fuji: 1976 and 1977. Suzuka: since 1987.

All the statistics go up to 31st December 2001.

The increase in the number of Grands Prix per year tends to shift the balance of some statistics: it is now easier to move up the order in some of the tables. However, this does not minimise the performances of drivers from the modern era.

Furthermore, the way points are allocated has changed several times since 1950.

- From 1950 to 1959: 8 points for 1st, 6 points for 2nd, 4 points for 3rd, 3 points for 4th, 2 points for 5th and 1 point for the driver setting the fastest lap.

- In 1960, the point for fastest lap was dropped, going instead to the 6th-placed driver.

- In 1961, the winner was given an extra point (9 points).

Since 1991, an additional point goes to the winner (10 points) to increase the value of the top slot.

# STATISTICS
## *1950-2001*

## FINAL CLASSIFICATION OF THE 2001 DRIVERS' WORLD CHAMPIONSHIP

| | | | Points |
|---|---|---|---|
| 1. | Michael Schumacher | (Ferrari) | 123 |
| 2. | David Coulthard | (McLaren-Mercedes) | 65 |
| 3. | Rubens Barrichello | (Ferrari) | 56 |
| 4. | Ralf Schumacher | (Williams-BMW) | 49 |
| 5. | Mika Häkkinen | (McLaren-Mercedes) | 37 |
| 6. | Juan Pablo Montoya | (Williams-BMW) | 31 |
| 7. | Jacques Villeneuve | (BAR Honda) | 12 |
| | Nick Heidfeld | (Sauber Petronas) | 12 |
| | Jarno Trulli | (Jordan Honda) | 12 |
| 10. | Kimi Räikkönen | (Sauber Petronas) | 9 |
| 11. | Giancarlo Fisichella | (Benetton Renault) | 8 |
| 12. | Eddie Irvine | (Jaguar) | 6 |
| | Heinz-Harald Frentzen | (Jordan Honda/Prost Acer) | 6 |
| 14. | Olivier Panis | (BAR Honda) | 5 |
| | Jean Alesi | (Prost Acer/Jordan Honda) | 5 |
| 16. | Pedro de la Rosa | (Jaguar) | 3 |
| 17. | Jenson Button | (Benetton Renault) | 2 |
| 18. | Jos Verstappen | (Arrows Asiatech) | 1 |

## FINAL CLASSIFICATION OF THE 2001 CONSTRUCTORS' WORLD CHAMPIONSHIP

| | Points | Poles | Wins |
|---|---|---|---|
| 1. Ferrari | 179 | 11 | 9 |
| 2. McLaren-Mercedes | 102 | 2 | 4 |
| 3. Williams-BMW | 80 | 4 | 4 |
| 4. Sauber-Petronas | 21 | 0 | 0 |
| 5. Jordan-Honda | 19 | 0 | 0 |
| 6. BAR-Honda | 17 | 0 | 0 |
| 7. Benetton-Renault | 10 | 0 | 0 |
| 8. Jaguar | 9 | 0 | 0 |
| 9. Prost-Acer | 4 | 0 | 0 |
| 10. Arrows-Asiatech | 1 | 0 | 0 |
| 11. Minardi-Fondmetal | 0 | 0 | 0 |

SCHUMI 2001 F1 CHAMPION

| 1950 | Guiseppe Farina | (Italy) | Alfa Romeo |
|------|-----------------|---------|------------|
| 1951 | Juan Manuel Fangio | (Argentina) | Alfa Romeo |
| 1952 | Alberto Ascari | (Italy) | Alfa Romeo |
| 1953 | Alberto Ascari | (Italy) | Alfa Romeo |
| 1954 | Juan Manuel Fangio | (Argentina) | Mercedes |
| 1955 | Juan Manuel Fangio | (Argentina) | Mercedes |
| 1956 | Juan Manuel Fangio | (Argentina) | Ferrari |
| 1957 | Juan Manuel Fangio | (Argentina) | Maserati |
| 1958 | Mike Hawthorn | (Great Britain) | Ferrari |
| 1959 | Jack Brabham | (Australia) | Cooper-Climax |
| 1960 | Jack Brabham | (Australia) | Cooper-Climax |
| 1961 | Phil Hill | (United States) | Ferrari |
| 1962 | Graham Hill | (Great Britain) | BRM |
| 1963 | Jim Clark | (Great Britain) | Lotus-Climax |
| 1964 | John Surtees | (Great Britain) | Ferrari |
| 1965 | Jim Clark | (Great Britain) | Lotus-Climax |
| 1966 | Jack Brabham | (Australia) | Brabham-Repco |
| 1967 | Dennis Hulme | (New Zealand) | Brabham-Repco |
| 1968 | Graham Hill | (Great Britain) | Lotus-Ford |
| 1969 | Jackie Stewart | (Great Britain) | Matra-Ford |
| 1970 | Jochen Rindt | (Austria) | Lotus-Ford |
| 1971 | Jackie Stewart | (Great Britain) | Tyrrell-Ford |
| 1972 | Emerson Fittipaldi | (Brazil) | Lotus-Ford |
| 1973 | Jackie Stewart | (Great Britain) | Tyrrell-Ford |
| 1974 | Emerson Fittipaldi | (Brazil) | McLaren-Ford |
| 1975 | Niki Lauda | (Austria) | Ferrari |
| 1976 | James Hunt | (Great Britain) | McLaren-Ford |
| 1977 | Niki Lauda | (Austria) | Ferrari |
| 1978 | Mario Andretti | (United States) | Lotus-Ford |
| 1979 | Jody Scheckter | (South Africa) | Ferrari |
| 1980 | Alan Jones | (Australia) | Williams-Ford |
| 1981 | Nelson Piquet | (Brazil) | Brabham-Ford |
| 1982 | Keke Rosberg | (Finland) | Williams-Ford |
| 1983 | Nelson Piquet | (Brazil) | Brabham-BMW |
| 1984 | Niki Lauda | (Austria) | McLaren-Tag-Porsche |
| 1985 | Alain Prost | (France) | McLaren-Tag-Porsche |
| 1986 | Alain Prost | (France) | McLaren-Tag-Porsche |
| 1987 | Nelson Piquet | (Brazil) | Williams-Honda |
| 1988 | Ayrton Senna | (Brazil) | McLaren-Honda |
| 1989 | Alain Prost | (France) | McLaren-Honda |
| 1990 | Ayrton Senna | (Brazil) | McLaren-Honda |
| 1991 | Ayrton Senna | (Brazil) | McLaren-Honda |
| 1992 | Nigel Mansell | (Great Britain) | Williams-Renault |
| 1993 | Alain Prost | (France) | Williams-Renault |
| 1994 | Michael Schumacher | (Germany) | Benetton-Ford |
| 1995 | Michael Schumacher | (Germany) | Benetton-Renault |
| 1996 | Damon Hill | (Great Britain) | Williams-Renault |
| 1997 | Jacques Villeneuve | (Canada) | Williams-Renault |
| 1998 | Mika Häkkinen | (Finland) | McLaren-Mercedes |
| 1999 | Mika Häkkinen | (Finland) | McLaren-Mercedes |
| 2000 | Michael Schumacher | (Germany) | Ferrari |
| 2001 | Michael Schumacher | (Germany) | Ferrari |

In 1958, a Formula 1 constructors' cup is established. In 1982, it becomes the Constructors' World Championship.

| 1958 | Vanwall | 1974 | McLaren | 1990 | McLaren |
|------|---------|------|---------|------|---------|
| 1959 | Cooper | 1975 | Ferrari | 1991 | McLaren |
| 1960 | Cooper | 1976 | Ferrari | 1992 | Williams |
| 1961 | Ferrari | 1977 | Ferrari | 1993 | Williams |
| 1962 | BRM | 1978 | Lotus | 1994 | Williams |
| 1963 | Lotus | 1979 | Ferrari |  |  |
| 1964 | Ferrari | 1980 | Williams | 1995 | Benetton |
| 1965 | Lotus | 1981 | Williams | 1996 | Williams |
| 1966 | Brabham | 1982 | Ferrari | 1997 | Williams |
| 1967 | Lotus | 1983 | Ferrari |  |  |
| 1968 | Lotus | 1984 | McLaren | 1998 | Mclaren |
| 1969 | Matra | 1985 | McLaren | 1999 | Ferrari |
| 1970 | Lotus | 1986 | Williams |  |  |
| 1971 | Tyrrell | 1987 | Williams | 2000 | Ferrari |
| 1972 | Lotus | 1988 | McLaren | 2001 | Ferrari |
| 1973 | Lotus | 1989 | McLaren |  |  |

| 5 titles: | Juan Manuel Fangio (Argentina) | 1951-1954-1955-1956-1957 |
|-----------|--------------------------------|--------------------------|
| 4 titles: | Alain Prost (France) | 1985-1986-1989-1993 |
|  | *Michael Schumacher (Germany)* | *1994-1995-2000-2001* |
| 3 titles: | Jack Brabham (Australia) | 1959-1960-1966 |
|  | Jackie Stewart (Great Britain) | 1969-1971-1973 |
|  | Niki Lauda (Austria) | 1975-1977-1984 |
|  | Nelson Piquet (Brazil) | 1981-1983-1987 |
|  | Ayrton Senna (Brazil) | 1988-1990-1991 |
| 2 titles: | Alberto Ascari (Italy) | 1952-1953 |
|  | Graham Hill (Great Britain) | 1962-1968 |
|  | Jim Clark (Great Britain) | 1963-1965 |
|  | Emerson Fittipaldi (Brazil) | 1972-1974 |
|  | Mika Häkkinen (Finland) | 1998-1999 |
| 1 title: | Giuseppe Farina (Italy) | 1950 |
|  | Mike Hawthorn (Great Britain) | 1958 |
|  | Phil Hill (United States) | 1961 |
|  | John Surtees (Great Britain) | 1964 |
|  | Dennis Hulme (New Zealand) | 1967 |
|  | Jochen Rindt (Austria) | 1970 |
|  | Mario Andretti (United States) | 1978 |
|  | Jody Scheckter (South Africa) | 1979 |
|  | Alan Jones (Australia) | 1980 |
|  | Keke Rosberg (Finland) | 1982 |
|  | Nigel Mansell (Great Britain) | 1992 |
|  | Damon Hill (Great Britain) | 1996 |
|  | *Jacques Villeneuve (Canada)* | *1997* |

## NUMBER OF GRANDS PRIX CONTESTED PER DRIVER

|  | |  | |
|---|---|---|---|
| R. Patrese | 256 | P. Alliot | 107 |
| G. Berger | 210 | J. Mass | 105 |
| A De Cesaris | 208 | J. Bonnier | 102 |
| N. Piquet | 204 | B. McLaren | 101 |
| J. Alesi | 201 | J. Stewart | 99 |
| A. Prost | 199 | *J. Villeneuve* | *99* |
| M. Alboreto | 194 | P. Diniz | 98 |
| N. Mansell | 187 | J. Siffert | 97 |
| G. Hill | 176 | C. Amon | 96 |
| J. Laffite | 176 | P. Depailler | 95 |
| N. Lauda | 171 | U. Katayama | 95 |
| T. Boutsen | 163 | I. Capelli | 94 |
| J. Herbert | 162 | M. Salo | 93 |
| *M. Schumacher* | *162* | J. Hunt | 92 |
| M. Häkkinen | 162 | *G. Fisichella* | *91* |
| A. Senna | 161 | J. Verstappen | 91 |
| M. Brundle | 158 | J.P. Beltoise | 86 |
| J. Watson | 152 | D. Gurney | 86 |
| R. Arnoux | 149 | J. Palmer | 84 |
| D. Warwick | 147 | *R. Schumacher* | *83* |
| *R. Barrichello* | *147* | M. Surer | 82 |
| C. Reutemann | 146 | M. Trintignant | 82 |
| E. Fittipaldi | 144 | *J. Trulli* | *80* |
| J.-P. Jarier | 132 | S. Johansson | 79 |
| E. Cheever | 132 | A. Nannini | 77 |
| C. Regazzoni | 132 | S. Nakajima | 74 |
| *E. Irvine* | *130* | V. Brambilla | 74 |
| *H.H. Frentzen* | *129* | M. Gugelmin | 74 |
| M. Andretti | 128 | H. Stuck | 74 |
| J. Brabham | 126 | J. Clark | 72 |
| *D. Coulthard* | *124* | C. Pace | 72 |
| R. Peterson | 123 | S. Modena | 70 |
| P. Martini | 119 | D. Pironi | 70 |
| J. Ickx | 116 | B. Giacomelli | 69 |
| A. Jones | 116 | G. Villeneuve | 67 |
| D. Hill | 116 | S. Moss | 66 |
| K. Rosberg | 114 | T. Fabi | 64 |
| P. Tambay | 114 | A. Suzuki | 64 |
| D. Hulme | 112 | J.J. Lehto | 62 |
| J. Scheckter | 112 | M. Blundell | 61 |
| J. Surtees | 111 | J. Rindt | 60 |
| E. De Angelis | 108 | G. Morbidelli | 60 |
| *O. Panis* | *108* | etc… | |

Author's note: In the 1950s and 1960s, the world championship was made up of less than ten races per year. Therefore, many well-known drivers do not feature in this classification.

|  | |  | |
|---|---|---|---|
| J.M. Fangio | 51 | G. Farina | 33 |
| M. Hailwood | 50 | A. Ascari | 32 |
| P. Hill | 48 | P. Collins | 32 |
| M. Hawthorn | 47 | W. Von Trips | 27 |
| L. Bandini | 42 | etc… | |
| T. Brooks | 38 | | |

## NUMBER OF POLE POSITIONS PER DRIVER

|  | |  | |
|---|---|---|---|
| A. Senna | 65 | P. Tambay | 5 |
| *M. Schumacher* | *43* | M. Hawthorn | 4 |
| J. Clark | 33 | D. Pironi | 4 |
| A. Prost | 33 | E. De Angelis | 3 |
| N. Mansell | 32 | T. Brooks | 3 |
| J.-M. Fangio | 28 | T. Fabi | 3 |
| M. Häkkinen | 26 | F. Gonzales | 3 |
| N. Lauda | 24 | D. Gurney | 3 |
| N. Piquet | 24 | J.P. Jarier | 3 |
| D. Hill | 20 | J. Scheckter | 3 |
| M. Andretti | 18 | *R. Barrichello* | *3* |
| R. Arnoux | 18 | *J.P. Montoya* | *3* |
| J. Stewart | 17 | M. Alboreto | 2 |
| S. Moss | 16 | J. Alesi | 2 |
| A. Ascari | 14 | *H.H. Frentzen* | *2* |
| J. Hunt | 14 | S. Lewis Evans | 2 |
| R. Peterson | 14 | J. Siffert | 2 |
| J. Brabham | 13 | G. Villeneuve | 2 |
| G. Hill | 13 | J. Watson | 2 |
| J. Ickx | 13 | L. Bandini | 1 |
| *J. Villeneuve* | *13* | J. Bonnier | 1 |
| G. Berger | 12 | T. Boutsen | 1 |
| *D. Coulthard* | *12* | V. Brambilla | 1 |
| J. Rindt | 10 | E. Castelloti | 1 |
| J. Surtees | 8 | P. Collins | 1 |
| R. Patrese | 8 | A. De Cesaris | 1 |
| J. Laffite | 7 | P. Depailler | 1 |
| E. Fittipaldi | 6 | *G. Fisichella* | *1* |
| P. Hill | 6 | B. Giacomelli | 1 |
| J.-P. Jabouille | 6 | D. Hulme | 1 |
| A. Jones | 6 | C. Pace | 1 |
| C. Reutemann | 6 | M. Parkes | 1 |
| C. Amon | 5 | T. Pryce | 1 |
| G. Farina | 5 | P. Revson | 1 |
| C. Regazzoni | 5 | W. Von Trips | 1 |
| K. Rosberg | 5 | *R. Schumacher* | *1* |

## NUMBER OF WINS PER DRIVER

|  | |  | |
|---|---|---|---|
| *M. Schumacher* | *53* | R. Schumacher | *3* |
| A. Prost | 51 | E. De Angelis | 2 |
| A. Senna | 41 | P. Depailler | 2 |
| N. Mansell | 31 | F. Gonzales | 2 |
| J. Stewart | 27 | J.-P. Jabouille | 2 |
| J. Clark | 25 | P. Revson | 2 |
| N. Lauda | 25 | P. Rodriguez | 2 |
| J.-M. Fangio | 24 | J. Siffert | 2 |
| N. Piquet | 23 | P. Tambay | 2 |
| D. Hill | 22 | M. Trintignant | 2 |
| M. Häkkinen | 20 | W. Von Trips | 2 |
| S. Moss | 16 | B. Vukovich | 2 |
| J. Brabham | 14 | J. Alesi | 1 |
| E. Fittipaldi | 14 | G. Baghetti | 1 |
| G. Hill | 14 | L. Bandini | 1 |
| A. Ascari | 13 | *R. Barrichello* | *1* |
| M. Andretti | 12 | J.-P. Beltoise | 1 |
| A. Jones | 12 | J. Bonnier | 1 |
| C. Reutemann | 12 | V. Brambilla | 1 |
| *J. Villeneuve* | *11* | J. Bryan | 1 |
| *D. Coulthard* | *11* | F. Cevert | 1 |
| J. Hunt | 10 | L. Fagioli | 1 |
| R. Peterson | 10 | P. Flaherty | 1 |
| J. Scheckter | 10 | P. Gethin | 1 |
| G. Berger | 10 | R. Ginther | 1 |
| D. Hulme | 8 | S. Hanks | 1 |
| J. Ickx | 8 | I. Ireland | 1 |
| R. Arnoux | 7 | J. Mass | 1 |
| T. Brooks | 6 | L. Musso | 1 |
| J. Laffite | 6 | *J P Montoya* | *1* |
| J. Rindt | 6 | A. Nannini | 1 |
| J. Surtees | 6 | G. Nilsson | 1 |
| G. Villeneuve | 6 | C. Pace | 1 |
| R. Patrese | 6 | *O. Panis* | *1* |
| M. Alboreto | 5 | J. Parsons | 1 |
| G. Farina | 5 | J. Rathman | 1 |
| C. Regazzoni | 5 | T. Ruttman | 1 |
| K. Rosberg | 5 | L. Scarfiotti | 1 |
| J. Watson | 5 | B. Sweikert | 1 |
| D. Gurney | 4 | P. Taruffi | 1 |
| B. McLaren | 4 | L. Wallard | 1 |
| T. Boutsen | 3 | R. Ward | 1 |
| P. Hill | 3 | | |
| M. Hawthorn | 3 | | |
| D. Pironi | 3 | | |
| *E. Irvine* | *3* | | |
| *H.H. Frentzen* | *3* | | |
| J. Herbert | 3 | | |

## NUMBER OF FASTEST RACE LAPS PER DRIVER

|  | |  | |  | |
|---|---|---|---|---|---|
| *M. Schumacher* | *44* | A. Jones | 13 | F. Gonzalez | 6 |
| A. Prost | 41 | R. Patrese | 13 | D. Gurney | 6 |
| N. Mansell | 30 | R. Arnoux | 12 | M. Hawthorn | 6 |
| J. Clark | 28 | A. Ascari | 11 | P. Hill | 6 |
| N. Lauda | 25 | J. Surtees | 11 | D. Pironi | 6 |
| M. Häkkinen | 24 | M. Andretti | 10 | J. Scheckter | 6 |
| J.-M. Fangio | 23 | J. Brabham | 10 | *H.H. Frentzen* | *6* |
| N. Piquet | 23 | G. Hill | 10 | *R. Schumacher* | *6* |
| G. Berger | 21 | D. Hulme | 9 | etc… | |
| S. Moss | 20 | R. Peterson | 9 | | |
| D. Hill | 19 | *J. Villeneuve* | *9* | | |
| A. Senna | 19 | J. Hunt | 8 | Of those still racing: | |
| *D. Coulthard* | *17* | J. Laffite | 7 | *R. Barrichello* | *3* |
| C. Regazzoni | 15 | G. Villeneuve | 7 | *J.P. Montoya* | *3* |
| J. Stewart | 15 | G. Farina | 6 | *G. Fisichella* | *1* |
| J. Ickx | 14 | E. Fittipaldi | 6 | *E. Irvine* | *1* |

## TOTAL POINTS SCORED PER DRIVER

| | | | |
|---|---|---|---|
| M. Schumacher | 801 | M. Andretti | 180 |
| A. Prost | 798,5 | J. Surtees | 180 |
| A. Senna | 614 | J. Hunt | 179 |
| N. Piquet | 485,5 | J. Watson | 169 |
| N. Mansell | 482 | H.H. Frentzen | 159 |
| N. Lauda | 420,5 | K. Rosberg | 159,5 |
| M. Häkkinen | 420 | P. Depailler | 141 |
| G. Berger | 386 | A. Ascari | 139 |
| J. Stewart | 360 | R. Schumacher | 135 |
| D. Hill | 360 | D. Gurney | 133 |
| D. Coulthard | 359 | T. Boutsen | 132 |
| C. Reutemann | 310 | G. Farina | 128,5 |
| G. Hill | 289 | M. Hawthorn | 127,5 |
| E. Fittipaldi | 281 | E. De Angelis | 122 |
| R. Patrese | 281 | J. Rindt | 109 |
| J.-M. Fangio | 277,51 | R. Ginther | 107 |
| J. Clark | 274 | G. Villeneuve | 107 |
| J. Brabham | 261 | P. Tambay | 103 |
| J. Scheckter | 259 | D. Pironi | 101 |
| J. Alesi | 241 | etc… | |
| J. Laffite | 228 | | |
| C. Regazzoni | 212 | **Of those still racing:** | |
| J. Villeneuve | 209 | G. Fisichella | 75 |
| A. Jones | 206 | O. Panis | 61 |
| R. Peterson | 206 | J. P. Montoya | 31 |
| B. McLaren | 196,5 | J. Trulli | 29 |
| R. Barrichello | 195 | J. Button | 14 |
| M. Alboreto | 186,5 | N. Heidfeld | 12 |
| S. Moss | 186,5 | K. Räikkönen | 9 |
| E. Irvine | 183 | P. de la Rosa | 6 |
| R. Arnoux | 181 | | |
| J. Ickx | 181 | | |

## THE PODIUM REGULARS

| | | | |
|---|---|---|---|
| A. Prost | 106 | R. Arnoux | 22 |
| M. Schumacher | 97 | G. Farina | 20 |
| A. Senna | 80 | J. Watson | 20 |
| N. Piquet | 60 | Ma. Andretti | 19 |
| N. Mansell | 59 | P. Depailler | 19 |
| N. Lauda | 54 | D. Gurney | 19 |
| M. Häkkinen | 51 | M. Hawthorn | 18 |
| D. Coulthard | 51 | A. Ascari | 17 |
| G. Berger | 48 | K. Rosberg | 17 |
| C. Reutemann | 45 | H.H. Frentzen | 16 |
| J. Stewart | 43 | T. Boutsen | 15 |
| D. Hill | 42 | F. Gonzales | 15 |
| R. Patrese | 37 | R. Schumacher | 14 |
| G. Hill | 36 | R. Ginther | 14 |
| J.M. Fangio | 35 | J.P. Beltoise | 13 |
| E. Fittipaldi | 35 | F. Cevert | 13 |
| D. Hulme | 33 | P. Hill | 13 |
| J. Scheckter | 33 | D. Pironi | 13 |
| J. Clark | 32 | J. Rindt | 13 |
| J. Laffite | 32 | G. Villeneuve | 13 |
| J. Brabham | 31 | C. Amon | 11 |
| J. Alesi | 31 | P. Tambay | 11 |
| C. Regazzoni | 28 | etc… | |
| B. McLaren | 27 | | |
| R. Peterson | 26 | **Of those still racing:** | |
| J. Ickx | 25 | G. Fisichella | 9 |
| E. Irvine | 25 | O. Panis | 6 |
| R. Barrichello | 25 | J. P. Montoya | 4 |
| A. Jones | 24 | M. Salo | 2 |
| S. Moss | 24 | N. Heidfeld | 1 |
| J. Surtees | 24 | J. Trulli | 1 |
| M. Alboreto | 23 | | |
| J. Hunt | 23 | | |
| J. Villeneuve | 23 | | |

## TOTAL KILOMETRES IN THE LEAD PER DRIVER

| | | | | | | | |
|---|---|---|---|---|---|---|---|
| M. Schumacher | 14318 | C. Reutemann | 3309 | C. Regazzoni | 1855 | R. Schumacher | 751 |
| A. Senna | 13613 | R. Peterson | 3304 | P. Hill | 1715 | H.H. Frentzen | 746 |
| A. Prost | 12575 | J. Hunt | 3229 | T. Brooks | 1525 | T. Boutsen | 662 |
| J. Clark | 10189 | J. Ickx | 3067 | D. Gurney | 1518 | J. Siffert | 636 |
| N. Mansell | 9642 | J. Villeneuve | 2970 | J. Laffite | 1476 | J. P. Montoya | 634 |
| J. Stewart | 9077 | A. Jones | 2877 | J. Alesi | 1285 | L. Bandini | 615 |
| N. Piquet | 7465 | J. Scheckter | 2837 | J. Watson | 1245 | P. Depailler | 614 |
| M. Häkkinen | 7201 | R. Patrese | 2571 | D. Pironi | 1238 | P. Rodriguez | 585 |
| N. Lauda | 7188 | R. Arnoux | 2561 | R. Barrichello | 979 | F. Cevert | 560 |
| D. Hill | 6248 | G. Villeneuve | 2244. | J.-P. Jabouille | 978 | J. Bonnier | 546 |
| G. Hill | 4618 | K. Rosberg | 2137 | P. Tambay | 975 | etc… | |
| J. Brabham | 4541 | J. Surtees | 2131 | M. Alboreto | 927 | | |
| D. Coulthard | 3669 | E. Fittipaldi | 2122 | E. Irvine | 838 | G. Fisichella | 172 |
| M. Andretti | 3577 | J. Rindt | 1905 | W. Von Trips | 787 | J. Trulli | 165 |
| G. Berger | 3456 | D. Hulme | 1900 | C. Amon | 784 | O. Panis | 53 |

## NUMBER OF LAPS IN THE LEAD PER DRIVER

| | | | | | | | |
|---|---|---|---|---|---|---|---|
| M. Schumacher | 3097 | G. Berger | 695 | J. Surtees | 310 | W. Von Trips | 156 |
| A. Senna | 2982 | J. Scheckter | 671 | D. Pironi | 295 | E. Irvine | 156 |
| A. Prost | 2705 | C. Reutemann | 648 | J. Watson | 287 | H.H. Frentzen | 149 |
| N. Mansell | 2099 | J. Hunt | 634 | J. Laffite | 279 | R. Schumacher | 148 |
| J. Clark | 2039 | J. Villeneuve | 634 | J. Alesi | 265 | J. Bonnier | 139 |
| J. Stewart | 1893 | A. Jones | 594 | M. Alboreto | 218 | L. Bandini | 136 |
| N. Lauda | 1620 | R. Patrese | 568 | R. Barrichello | 210 | J. Siffert | 122 |
| N. Piquet | 1572 | G. Villeneuve | 533 | P. Tambay | 197 | J. P. Montoya | 122 |
| M. Häkkinen | 1490 | J. Ickx | 529 | D. Gurney | 191 | J.-P. Beltoise | 101 |
| D. Hill | 1352 | R. Arnoux | 506 | P. Hill | 189 | etc… | |
| G. Hill | 1073 | K. Rosberg | 506 | J.-P. Jabouille | 184 | | |
| J. Brabham | 827 | E. Fittipaldi | 459 | C. Amon | 183 | **Of those still racing:** | |
| M. Andretti | 799 | D. Hulme | 436 | T. Brooks | 173 | J. Trulli | 38 |
| D. Coulthard | 760 | J. Rindt | 387 | P. Depailler | 165 | G. Fisichella | 35 |
| R. Peterson | 706 | C. Regazzoni | 361 | T. Boutsen | 164 | O. Panis | 16 |

This shows the ability of a driver to finish the greatest number of Grands Prix in the course of a season. This statistic does not include the Indianapolis 500 Miles race, which was included in the Formula 1 world championship from 1951 to 1960.

| | | | | |
|---|---|---|---|---|
| 1. | J. Clark | 1963 | Lotus | 10/10 |
| 2. | R. Ginther | 1964 | BRM | 10/10 |
| 3. | G. Hill | 1962 | BRM | 9/9 |
| 4. | M. Hawthorn | 1953 | Ferrari | 8/8 |
| 5. | J.M. Fangio | 1954 | Maserati & Mercedes | 8/8 |
| 6. | D. Gurney | 1961 | Porsche | 8/8 |
| 7. | J. Alesi | 2001 | Prost & Jordan | 16/17 |
| 8. | A. Senna | 1991 | McLaren | 15/16 |
| 9. | A. Prost | 1993 | Williams | 15/16 |
| 10. | E. Irvine | 1999 | Ferrari | 15/16 |
| 11. | D. Hulme | 1973 | McLaren | 14/15 |
| 12. | M. Schumacher | 2001 | Ferrari | 15/17 |
| 13. | J. Laffite | 1978 | Ligier | 14/16 |
| 14. | A. Senna | 1988 | McLaren | 14/16 |
| 15. | A. Prost | 1988 | McLaren | 14/16 |
| 16. | M. Alboreto | 1992 | Footwork | 14/16 |
| 17. | O. Panis | 1994 | Ligier | 14/16 |
| 18. | J. Alesi | 1997 | Benetton | 14/17 |
| 19. | M. Häkkinen | 2000 | McLaren | 14/17 |
| 20. | D. Coulthard | 2000 | McLaren | 14/17 |

etc...

As an anecdote to illustrate this statistic, consistency was not the greatest strength of Italian driver Andrea de Cesaris. From the 1985 French Grand Prix to the 1988 race in Mexico, he only saw the chequered flag 3 times from 41 starts…
He holds a famous record: 19 consecutive retirements and non-qualifications from the 1985 French Grand Prix to the 1986 Mexican Grand Prix.

## NUMBER OF WORLD CHAMPIONSHIP TITLES PER COUNTRY

**12 titles:**
GREAT BRITAIN:
Hawthorn (1), G. Hill (2), Clark (2), Surtees (1), Stewart (3), Hunt (1), Mansell (1), D. Hill (1)

**8 titles:**
BRAZIL: E. Fittipaldi (2), Piquet (3), Senna (3)

**5 titles:**
ARGENTINA: Fangio (5)

**4 titles:**
AUSTRALIA: Brabham (3), Jones (1)
AUSTRIA: Rindt (1), Lauda (3)
FRANCE: Prost (4)
GERMANY: M. Schumacher (4)

**3 titles:**
ITALY: Farina (1), Ascari (2)
FINLAND: Rosberg (1), Häkkinen (2)

**2 titles:**
UNITED STATES: P. Hill (1), M. Andretti (1)

**1 title:**
NEW ZEALAND: Hulme (1)
SOUTH AFRICA: Scheckter (1)
CANADA: J. Villeneuve (1)

*(Number of titles)

## CONSTRUCTORS' WORLD CHAMPIONSHIP: NUMBER OF TITLES

**11 titles:**
Ferrari 1961, 64, 75, 76, 77, 79, 82, 83, 99, 2000, 2001
**9 titles:**
Williams 1981, 82, 86, 87, 92, 93, 94, 96, 97
**8 titles:**
McLaren 1974, 84, 85, 88, 89, 90, 91, 98
**7 titles:**
Lotus 1963, 65, 68, 70, 72, 73, 78
**2 titles:**
Cooper 1959, 60
Brabham 1966, 67
**1 title:**
Vanwall 1958
BRM 1962
Matra 1969
Tyrrell 1971
Benetton 1995

## CONSTRUCTORS' WORLD CHAMPIONSHIP: NUMBER OF WINS

| | | | |
|---|---|---|---|
| *Ferrari* | 144 | Mercedes | 9 |
| *McLaren* | 134 | Vanwall | 9 |
| *Williams* | 107 | Ligier | 9 |
| Lotus | 79 | March | 3 |
| Brabham | 35 | Wolf | 3 |
| Benetton | 26 | *Jordan* | 3 |
| Tyrrell | 23 | Honda | 2 |
| BRM | 17 | Hesketh | 1 |
| Cooper | 16 | Penske | 1 |
| *Renault* | 15 | Porsche | 1 |
| Alfa Romeo | 10 | Shadow | 1 |
| Maserati | 9 | Stewart | 1 |
| Matra | 9 | | |

## CONSTRUCTORS' WORLD CHAMPIONSHIP: NUMBER OF POLE POSITIONS

| | | | |
|---|---|---|---|
| *Ferrari* | 148 | Mercedes | 8 |
| *McLaren* | 112 | Vanwall | 7 |
| *Williams* | 112 | March | 5 |
| Lotus | 107 | Matra | 4 |
| Brabham | 39 | Shadow | 3 |
| *Renault* | 31 | Lancia | 2 |
| Benetton | 16 | *Jordan* | 2 |
| Tyrrell | 14 | *Arrows* | 1 |
| Alfa Romeo | 12 | Honda | 1 |
| BRM | 11 | Lola | 1 |
| Cooper | 11 | Porsche | 1 |
| Maserati | 10 | Wolf | 1 |
| Ligier | 9 | Stewart | 1 |

## CONSTRUCTORS' WORLD CHAMPIONSHIP: NUMBER OF GRANDS PRIX CONTESTED

| | | | |
|---|---|---|---|
| Ferrari | 653 | Jordan | 180 |
| McLaren | 526 | Sauber | 147 |
| Lotus | 490 | Osella | 132 |
| Williams | 445 | Cooper | 129 |
| Tyrrell | 418 | Larrousse | 126 |
| Brabham | 399 | Lola | 125 |
| Arrows | 371 | Renault | 123 |
| Ligier | 326 | Surtees | 117 |
| Benetton | 317 | etc... | |
| Minardi | 271 | Prost | 83 |
| March | 230 | BAR | 50 |
| BRM | 197 | Jaguar | 34 |

## CONSTRUCTORS' WORLD CHAMPIONSHIP: NUMBER OF POINTS SCORED

| | | | |
|---|---|---|---|
| Ferrari | 2692,5 | March | 171,5 |
| McLaren | 2583,5 | Arrows | 165 |
| Williams | 2111,5 | Matra | 155 |
| Lotus | 1352 | Sauber | 110 |
| Benetton | 877,5 | Wolf | 79 |
| Brabham | 854,5 | Shadow | 67,5 |
| Tyrrell | 617 | etc... | |
| BRM | 439 | | |
| Ligier | 390 | BAR | 37 |
| Cooper | 333 | Prost | 35 |
| Renault | 312 | Minardi | 28 |
| Jordan | 249 | Jaguar | 13 |

## NUMBER OF CONSTRUCTOR TITLES PER ENGINE MANUFACTURER

**11 titles:**
Ferrari: 1961, 64, 75, 76, 77, 79, 82, 83, 99, 2000, 2001.

**10 titles:**
Ford: 1968, 69, 70, 71, 72, 73, 74, 78, 80, 81.

**6 titles:**
Honda: 1986, 87, 88, 89, 90, 91.
Renault: 1992, 93, 94, 95, 96, 97.

**4 titles:**
Climax: 1959, 60, 63, 65.

**2 titles:**
Repco: 1966, 67.
TAG-Porsche: 1984, 85.

**1 title:**
Vanwall: 1958.
BRM: 1962.
Mercedes: 1998.

## NUMBER OF WINS PER TYRE MANUFACTURER

| | | | |
|---|---|---|---|
| GoodYear | 368 | Firestone | 49 |
| Dunlop | 83 | Pirelli | 45 |
| Michelin | 63 | Continental | 10 |
| Bridgestone | 55 | | |

## NUMBER OF WINS PER ENGINE MANUFACTURER

| | | | |
|---|---|---|---|
| Ford | 174 | BMW | 13 |
| Ferrari | 144 | Alfa Romeo | 12 |
| Renault | 95 | Maserati | 11 |
| Honda | 72 | Vanwall | 9 |
| Climax | 40 | Repco | 8 |
| Mercedes | 39 | Mugen-Honda | 4 |
| Porsche | 26 | Matra | 3 |
| TAG Turbo | 25 | Porsche | 1 |
| BRM | 18 | Weslake | 1 |

## NUMBER OF POLE POSITIONS PER ENGINE MANUFACTURER

| | | | |
|---|---|---|---|
| Ferrari | 148 | Repco | 7 |
| Ford | 137 | TAG Turbo | 7 |
| Renault | 136 | Vanwall | 7 |
| Honda | 74 | Matra | 4 |
| Climax | 44 | Hart | 2 |
| Mercedes | 41 | Lancia | 2 |
| BMW | 19 | Mecachrome | 1 |
| Alfa Romeo | 15 | Mugen-Honda | 1 |
| BRM | 11 | Porsche | 1 |
| Maserati | 11 | | |

## NUMBER OF GRANDS PRIX CONTESTED PER ENGINE MANUFACTURER

| | | | |
|---|---|---|---|
| Ferrari | 653 | Peugeot | 132 |
| Ford | 517 | BMW | 125 |
| Renault | 303 | Petronas | 83 |
| Honda | 236 | Supertec | 49 |
| Alfa Romeo | 212 | Mugen-Honda | 47 |
| BRM | 197 | Asiatech | 17 |
| Mercedes | 153 | etc... | |

## CONSTRUCTORS' WORLD CHAMPIONSHIP: NUMBER OF FASTEST LAPS

| | | | |
|---|---|---|---|
| Ferrari | 147 | Mercedes | 11 |
| Williams | 118 | March | 7 |
| McLaren | 107 | Vanwall | 6 |
| Lotus | 70 | Surtees | 4 |
| Brabham | 41 | Jordan | 2 |
| Benetton | 38 | Eagle | 2 |
| Tyrrell | 20 | Honda | 2 |
| Renault | 18 | Shadow | 2 |
| BRM | 15 | Wolf | 2 |
| Maserati | 15 | Ensign | 1 |
| Alfa Romeo | 14 | Gordini | 1 |
| Cooper | 13 | Hesketh | 1 |
| Matra | 12 | Lancia | 1 |
| Ligier | 11 | Parnelli | 1 |

## RECORD FOR NUMBER OF POINTS SCORED BY A CONSTRUCTOR IN A SINGLE SEASON

| | |
|---|---|
| McLaren 199 points in 1988 | McLaren 156 points in 1998 |
| Ferrari 179 points in 2001 | McLaren 143,5 points in 1984 |
| Williams 175 points in 1986 | McLaren 141 points in 1989 |
| Ferrari 170 points in 2000 | Williams 141 points in 1986 |
| Williams 168,5 points in 1993 | Benetton 137 points in 1995 etc... |
| Williams 164 points in 1992 | |

## NUMBER OF DRIVER WORLD CHAMPIONSHIP TITLES PER ENGINE MANUFACTURER

**13 titles:**
Ford Cosworth:
1968, 69, 70, 71, 72, 73, 74, 76, 78, 80, 81, 82, 94.

**11 titles:**
Ferrari:
1952, 53, 56, 58, 61, 64, 75, 77, 79, 2000, 2001.

**5 titles:**
Honda:
1987, 88, 89, 90, 91.

Renault:
1992, 93, 95, 96, 97.

**4 titles:**
Climax: 1959, 60, 63, 65.
Mercedes:
1954, 55, 98, 99.

**3 titles:**
TAG-Porsche: 1984, 85, 86.

**2 titles:**
Alfa Romeo: 1950, 51.
Maserati: 1954, 57.
Repco: 1966, 67.

**1 title:**
BRM: 1962.
BMW turbo: 1983.